Rationalism and Emancipation in Psychoanalysis:

The Work of Jean Laplanche

by Hélène Tessier

Translated by Jonathan House and Andrew Baird

New York:
The Unconscious in Translation

Original French version:

Rationalisme et Émancipation en Psychanalyse: L'Œuvre de Jean Laplanche ISBN 978-2-13-062459-2

ISSN 2103-4893

Dépot légal – 1re édition : 2014, avril

© Presses Universitaires de France, 2014 6, avenue Reille, 75014 Paris

Cover art: "Circles in a Circle," Vasily Kandinsky

1923, oil on canvas

Philadelphia Museum of Art,

The Louise and Walter Arensberg Collection, 1950-134-104

ISBN 978-1-942254-14-0

Library of Congress Control Number: 2020931545

CONTENTS

Introduction

La dégradation de la raison,
voilà la racine du mal, la plus profonde.
—V. Klemperer, *Je veux témoigner jusqu'au bout:*
Journal 1942–1945

It has become difficult be involved with psychoanalysis without grappling with its definition. In psychoanalytic circles, the debate on this question is largely hidden, thanks to the postmodern cultural conditions that favor eclecticism and easily accommodate a growing conceptual flux. Nevertheless, the question of definition arises forcefully when it comes to determining the place of psychoanalysis within the many diverse disciplines and therapeutic approaches that are also concerned with phenomena of the soul. It is also essential to discussions of the contribution of psychoanalysis to the understanding of emotional disorders. Finally, the question of definition is central in determining what psychoanalysis can bring to thought and action in the social field.

In the present context, demonstrating the importance of psychoanalysis—or generating interest in psychoanalysis—can quickly become meaningless if one does not specify what one means by "psychoanalysis." For instance, could we seriously argue that Lacanian approaches are examples of the same conception of psychoanalysis as that embodied in relational approaches based on attachment theory? Moreover, when other disciplines seek to integrate psychoanalysis into the understanding of the issues in their field, to what do they refer? In this regard, invoking a common ground of clinical practice is not convincing, unless one is persuaded that theory has no influence on practice, a position that is, to say the least, debatable. The decline of interest in psychoanalysis should not be allowed to force analysts to close ranks around the term "psychoanalysis" if the term no longer corresponds to a shared reality. And if such a reality really does exist, what is it, and how can we judge whether it deserves our support?

Laplanche's work addresses the epistemological problems confronting psychoanalysis directly. It cannot be inserted into contemporary psychoanalytic eclecticism, and this characteristic is one of its most distinctive traits. In fact, Laplanche's thought involves a demand for coherence that makes it a polemical interlocutor of each of the principal contemporary orientations. Laplanche's theory is grounded on Freud's discovery, but nevertheless remains an original theory that distances itself from Freudian theory in important respects, particularly from the direction taken by Freud's final syntheses. Laplanche has redefined several fundamental psychoanalytic concepts. Notably, he has questioned the role that Freud attributes to phylogenesis, to "biological bedrock," to sexual difference, and to considering the major complexes as originary contents of the unconscious. Laplanche has also denounced definitions of the unconscious and of sexuality that postulate an endogenous origin for the drives. Thus, in many respects, Laplanche's theory is in opposition to the dominant currents of contemporary psychoanalysis.[1]

That tells us nothing about the value of Laplanche's theory or about the reasons for preferring it to another theory. If we must choose how to define the psychoanalytic field and its principal concepts, what criteria should determine our choices? Laplanche's thought falls within the rationalist tradition. This affiliation—seen

---

1 See Hélène Tessier, "Jean Laplanche in Rational Perspective: Translation as a Basic Anthropological Situation in Psychoanalysis," *Revue canadienne de psychanalyse* 18, no. 2 (2010): 281–329. viii

in the general theory of seduction (GTS) and in the links proposed between that theory and the mode of action of psychoanalysis—constitutes one of the criteria that help establish this theory's validity. That is the thesis of this book.

This thesis is based on two postulates. First it entails the recognition that a theory's philosophical affiliation—and this is notably true for a psychoanalytic theory—allows not only for a better understanding of the theory but also for an appreciation of its ethical dimensions. Furthermore, it assumes that ethical references play an essential role in epistemological reflection and that in the human sciences the compatibility of a theory with the values of justice and respect for human dignity is among the criteria for the validation and the validity of the theory.

This book is also based on the conviction that psychoanalysis can contribute in a specific way to reflection in the social field and that, because its object is the sexual unconscious, psychoanalysis occupies a place that cannot be filled by other disciplines. Nevertheless, this object must be defined in a way that can allow the emergence of the complementarity of psychoanalysis with these other disciplines and can reveal epistemological choices that do not pull these disciplines away from a demand for truth that should guide their own projects.

Chapter 1 deals with the rationalist affiliation of Laplanche's thought and describes its principal manifestations as they appear in the GTS. It also confronts these manifestations of rationalism with the dominant epistemological choices of contemporary psychoanalysis. Chapter 2 presents the principal concepts of the GTS and of the translational hypothesis of repression—the two faces of Laplanche's theory—while showing how they are linked to the rationalist tradition. Chapter 3 discusses the rationalist tradition as defined in this book. The definition is specific to this book, taking its inspiration principally from literary sources, especially from Thomas Mann and Victor Klemperer, but it is also inspired by the philosophical thought of Lukács. Chapter 3 also examines the form adopted by irrationalist tendencies in contemporary psychoanalysis and the problems that they raise. Chapter 4 discusses specific aspects of Laplanche's thought in relation to rationalism in psychoanalysis, notably to the concepts of alienation and subjectivity. In that discussion, the chapter establishes certain parallels with the Marxist theory of reification and with the Hegelian thought that bears on the movement from consciousness to self-consciousness. The book ends by recalling the importance of the theory of translation in the rationalist affiliation of Laplanche's thought and in the conception of truth upon which Laplanche's thought is based.

To understand the object of psychoanalysis and its role among other disciplines, "it is necessary to relate it to a wide-ranging reflection on the meanings, the conditions, and the ends of human action."[2] Laplanche's thought lends itself particularly well to such an exercise: In it, philosophical work is inseparable from a profound respect for what, in the human being, can keep alive the aim of transformation.

---

2 M. Freitag, *Le Naufrage de l'université* (Quebec: 1998), 81.

1

A Copernican Psychoanalysis: Laplanche's Theory and the Epistemological Choices in Psychoanalysis

Laplanche's psychoanalytic theory is grounded on a deep knowledge of Freud's work. It rests upon the fundamental achievements of psychoanalysis, namely the discovery of the unconscious and the recognition of sexuality's centrality among the determinants of human thought and behavior. At the same time, because of its epistemological orientation and the philosophical tradition to which it is linked, it positions itself in opposition to the main post-Freudian orientations.

Laplanche's thought reveals a specific conception of the soul and of psychoanalysis, psychoanalysis being understood as a theory of the soul and as a transformative practice. The use of the term "soul" is not an accident but a purposeful theoretical choice. The word "soul" makes up part of Laplanche's theory and constitutes a central point, both of his epistemology and of his conception of the human being. In his translation of Freud and in his own texts, Laplanche opts for the terms "âme" and "*animique*" to render the German terms "*Seele*" and "*seelisch*" even though French translations traditionally use the terms "*psyché*," "*psychisme*," and "*psychique*."[3] Psychoanalytic writings in French continue to refer to these latter terms, and the usage of "âme" in a psychoanalytic context generally gives rise to a certain uneasiness. For their part, English translations have opted for "mind" and "mental" or sometimes, depending on

---

3 A. Bourguignon et al., *Traduire Freud* (Paris: Presses Universitaires de France, 1989), 77–78.

the context, "psychic" and "psychical." The term *"Seele"* refers back to a philosophical tradition holding not only that the soul is a more expansive entity than the mind [*esprit*] but also that in French it is not reducible to the generally accepted meaning of the word *"psyché"* or to the technical sense the term has acquired. The use of the word and the concept of soul in Laplanche's theory is a link to a rationalist tradition expressed eloquently in the writings of Thomas Mann, for whom the opposition of soul and mind is just as problematic as that of soul and body.

Psychoanalytic observation has brought to light a new understanding of the fact that humans, often despite themselves, do not always act in their own best interest. To various degrees, they act in self-destructive ways. They repeat the same mistakes. They often seem possessed by contradictory and conflictual desires that, although these desires are clearly embodied in the consequences of their actions and decisions, they, in good faith, have difficulty acknowledging as their own. Psychoanalysis is born out of the observation that the ego is not the master of its own house and is in large part driven by forces that appear foreign to the ego itself. These forces, which are resistant to education, to personal effort, and to good intentions, cannot be reduced to a theory of needs and motivation. For psychoanalytic theory, these forces constitute manifestations of the sexual unconscious, a dynamic unconscious that is not directly observable and whose action is recognized through its derivative effects.

Although, over the course of his theorizing, Freud several times reworked both the definition of the sexual unconscious and its role in the human soul, nevertheless, the idea that the mode of action of the unconscious is a result of a logic other than that of intentionality[4]

---

4 Here, the term "intentionality" is used in Brentano's sense: It is used as a criterion that permits distinguishing physical facts from psychic facts. According

remained a guiding thread of Freudian theory and practice. This point permits us to affirm that the initial project of psychoanalysis is linked to the rationalist tradition, because for Freud it was not a question of denying the irrational aspects of the soul or of human behavior but precisely of recognizing their existence and providing a rational account of them, trying to explain them by elucidating their determining factors.

The affiliation of Laplanche's theory with the rationalist tradition begins, therefore, with the links that Freudian thought and the initial aim of psychoanalysis had with this tradition. Laplanche's theory is built on the epistemological questions posed by the contradictions in Freud's work, notably at those moments when Freud distanced himself from the demands of rationalism in his attempt to account for the unconscious and sexuality by using of the notion of phylogenesis and by biologizing the drive. What's more, these elements of Freudian theory that rest on an irrationalist foundation are precisely those that constitute the basis of the main post-Freudian orientations. These orientations have completed the rupture between psychoanalytic theory and the rationalist tradition—indeed, there is scarcely any trace of that tradition in the dominant currents of post-Freudian thought.

What is proposed here refers to a definition of rationalism that will be developed in chapter 3. This definition involves both a political conception and a philosophical analysis. It considers rationalism to be a bulwark against the various forms of obscurantism that nourish totalitarianism. Without, at this point, elaborating the political and moral stakes of rationalism as they are defined in this work, it is appropriate to present some of its characteristics here.

Rationalism should not be confused with the exclusive usage

---

to Brentano, every psychic fact is intentional; in other words, every psychic fact relates to an object.

of understanding, or with a superficial understanding of the rationality of thought and behavior, or with the rational character of the exposition of a thesis or a theory. As we have just emphasized, rationalism demands that one recognizes the soul's irrational aspects, without considering them as facts inaccessible to reason. In psychoanalysis, this consists in the recognition of a reality that exists independently of and irreducible to our consciousness: the reality of the sexual unconscious. It also entails the exercise of critical thought to question the foundational and nonhistorical character that psychoanalysis attributes to the content of the unconscious, or to myths and the mythical use of anatomy, or, in other psychoanalytic orientations, to psychological subjectivity. Finally, rationalism involves a demand for truth, and that presupposes accepting that truth exists, including when determining truth is determines a choice between psychoanalytic concepts.

The chapter's goal is to present the main characteristics of Laplanche's theory, their links to the rationalist tradition, and their relation to the epistemological problems raised by contemporary psychoanalysis. It will examine, on the one hand, how Laplanche's theory distinguishes itself both from Freudian theory and from the major trends in today's psychoanalytic theorizing and, on the other hand, how it facilitates building a bridge between psychoanalysis and the social field.

1. Psychoanalysis and the Social Field

Why take an interest in psychoanalysis today? This is not a rhetorical question. Psychoanalysis is losing momentum both as a method of treatment and as theory. What's more, it doesn't always help itself with the relative success it enjoys in certain milieu when it pronounces upon psychological, social, political, or even cultural questions. Too often psychoanalysis becomes synonymous with normative positions on familial relations or with mythical, stereotypical explanations of human relations. Finally, as a modality of treatment, it has tended to distinguish itself less and less from other modalities of psychotherapeutic intervention.[5]

a) Relations between Psychoanalysis and the Social Sciences: The Path of Rationalism

Nevertheless, the contribution of psychoanalysis is indispensable to understanding human behavior. Because it is not the only discipline that studies phenomena of the soul, the contribution of psychoanalysis depends on its ability to delimit its own epistemological field. Psychology, theology, philosophy, neurology, psychiatry, biology, the cognitive sciences, and sociology also address those phenomena. What's more, psychoanalysis shares the field of psychotherapy with psychiatry, psychology, and other approaches, notably pastoral ones, which historically have played a major role in the development of "talking cures" in the United States.[6] However, psychoanalysis is the only discipline that posits a sexual unconscious and makes it the object of its study.

The relationship between psychoanalysis and the social sciences insofar as there is one—and, more generally, between psychoanalysis and the human sciences—presupposes that the concept of the unconscious be taken into consideration in the fields of study of those sciences. For this to be a true relationship, and not simply the description of parallels that might be of interest to a given researcher, a link between the unconscious and the objects of research of the human sciences must already exist. This link is found in the hybrid forms in which derivatives of the sexual unconscious

5 Peter Fonagy, "Some Complexities in the Relationship of Psychoanalytic Theory to Technique," *Pych. Quat.* 72, no. 1 (January 2003): 13–47.

6 Hélène Tessier, *La psychanalyse americaine* (Paris: Presses Universitaires de France, 2005).

appear. Such derivatives manifest themselves in phenomena and attitudes that are among the objects of study of the other sciences, for example: the propensity for conformism, fascination with power, submission to authority, selfdestructive behaviors, the force of fantasies and their influence not only on the health or mood of individuals but also on economic and social relations. The identification of the relationship between the unconscious and the domains studied by the human sciences, as well as a demonstration that the relationship is not contingent but essential, proceeds from a rationalist postulate. The relationship is linked to rationalism by two factors: the category of totality and the unity of theory and practice.

The Category of Totality

By positing a sexual unconscious as a force that reveals itself to the individual—most often a posteriori—as a strange and foreign power, psychoanalysis has formulated a concept, but it did not invent the reality the concept describes. This reality acts outside and independently of psychoanalysis, both at the individual level and at the level of social relations. This is why, without replacing the contributions of other disciplines, psychoanalysis allows both matter specific to individuals and social relations to be grasped from a different angle. In learning, for example, in addition to cognitive and emotional factors, other forces need to be taken into account, forces that produces attitudes pulling the subject in directions opposed to the desired result. These forces resist cognitive and behavioral interventions and are not necessarily dissipated during the exploration of emotional states.

An example from the field of conflict resolution: Can one seriously believe that negotiations are based only on the interests of the parties or on what is called a "rational" calculation of interests? Is there always only one rational approach for each side? The tendency to submission, the subtle play of power relations, the success of explicit intimidation, cannot be explained solely by social psychology, the theory of needs, or sociology. Each of these disciplines has legitimacy, but none of them, nor even all of them together, can claim to give a complete account of the negotiation. Neither can psychoanalysis. However, at a minimum, the psychoanalytic perspective on the sexual unconscious, especially the central place psychoanalysis gives to sadistic and masochistic fantasies, permits descriptions of negotiations to give a more complete picture of what is at stake, including goals that, if less apparent, may be active in the situation. This perspective can also help guard against approaches to negotiation that appear neutral, but that ultimately favor the stronger party.

One could give several examples taken from other fields of activity, notably from psychotherapy. From the psychoanalytic perspective, the sexual unconscious is at work in all human behavior. If one wants to give an account of the full reality of any human situation, taking account of the nature and modes of action of the sexual unconscious is not a matter of preference but a necessity.

Although the action of the unconscious can be found in each of the factors that determine human behavior and it is not simply chance that links the effects of the unconscious to these factors, it is necessary and legitimate to study specific phenomena of unconscious action using the unconscious's own terms. In this case, however, it is important to recognize that one is not describing the whole reality of the object being studied. The whole does not correspond to the sum of the parts: It must be admitted that, at least in the sciences that involve human reality, each part of the whole modifies every other part—they are tied together by dynamic relationships.

The Unity of Theory and Practice

The question of the whole also arises in the relationship between theory and practice. The rationalist tradition, notably its dialectical version, was concerned with the conditions necessary for thought to transform reality. These conditions are found at the moment when theory and practice come together, a moment that itself leads back to the problem of totality.

For thought to have an effect on practice, for thought to be able to transform reality, it must have access to reality. It must be able to think of reality as a concrete reality, since, by definition, the real to be transformed is necessarily concrete—otherwise it would not be real. However, reaching reality by way of thought does not happen automatically. Contrary to what one might believe, the concrete cannot be grasped directly without mediation. It constitutes a synthesis of many determinants. For the thought of reality to be effective— and here we are speaking of theory—it must be able to encompass the whole of reality. A partial reality remains an abstraction. It is a thought about reality and not reality itself. This is why Paul Ricœur, when defining the dialectic, evoked "a procedure whereby reflection overcomes its own abstraction, in order to make itself complete, that is to say, concrete."[7]

The necessity of attaining a complete reflection implies that, even when one studies partial aspects of a situation—which is inevitable in a specific field of study—one does not eliminate the horizon of a reality that, to be concrete, must be grasped in its totality and neither broken up arbitrarily nor unified on a contingent basis. Such a perspective also belongs to the rationalist tradition. As such, Friedrich von Schiller defined true rationalism as that which led to authentic freedom of thought through its capacity to resist both "the arbitrariness of connections" and "the brutality of

---

7 Ricœur, *De l'interprétation* (Paris: Seuil, 1965), 361.

distinctions."[8] These terms express how, in Schiller's view, totality is embodied in rationalism. In opposition to empiricism, which, in this account, considers only an isolated aspect of the totality of experience, rationalism "must embrace the totality." In so doing, it must be careful not to mistake plurality for totality.

Today, the term "totality" is treated with suspicion. It is easily discredited because of its association with the term "totalitarian." The demand for totality is a central theme of Marxist dialectics. Whatever one thinks of it, "totality" is not a synonym for "totalitarian." It does not mean that it is necessary to force an object into intellectual categories that resist it, but, on the contrary, it implies the obligation to avoid arbitrary distinctions that the mind could make "to the detriment of the object."[9] In other words, the category of totality demands that one consider the object or phenomenon in question in the fullness of its determinants, including its origins and its consequences,[10] to move in the direction of the concrete conception Ricœur described as "thought's final frontier."[11] What are the benefits of this exercise? Why is it so important? Because it is the necessary condition for theory to have a transformative impact on reality. Such a stage corresponds to the moment of unity of theory and practice described above. Theory can only transform the real if it has access to it. The moment when thought is brought to bear on concrete reality—that is to say, on the object in all of its

---

8 Schiller to Goethe, January 19, 1798, in *Correspondence 1794–1805*, trans. L. Herr (Paris: Gallimard, 1994), 26–27.

9 Ibid., 27.

10 To give an example from the legal sphere: The independence of the judiciary remains an abstract reality if one limits oneself to examining the separation of powers in constitutional law and the independence of judges within the court system. Concrete independence implies looking at several other aspects, such as recruitment pools, method of appointment, career development, class membership, gender, networks of influences, social relations of work, etc.

11 Ricœur, *De l'interprétation*, 361.

aspects, including its historical aspects—is the moment when reality is grasped by thought. In other cases, thought is brought to bear on a representation of reality, and in these cases, the relationship between theory and practice is different.

b) Laplanche's Theory and the Unity of Theory and Practice

It is not only in the social sciences that a perspective on reality as a totality is necessary. Psychoanalysis cannot do without it. It must delimit its object in such a way that it foregrounds a specific conception of the soul in its relation to the object of psychoanalysis. Laplanche's theory addresses this requirement. For Laplanche, psychoanalysis's object is the sexual unconscious and the ways of accessing it, this defined in the Freudian sense of the dynamic unconscious as that force that escapes the logic of meaning and communication and that, for the most part, constitutes the "material cause" of our actions, thoughts, and emotions.[12]

The relationship between theory and practice is central for psychoanalysis. Psychoanalysis is not a theoretical discipline but a theory of practice. When, in 1937,[13] Freud categorizes psychoanalysis, along with teaching and governing, as an "impossible profession," he highlights the goal of transformation that is central to these activities.

Psychoanalysis is a practice of transformation.

According to Laplanche, there is no opposition between psychoanalysis as knowledge and psychoanalysis as therapeutic practice.[14] This position is based on postulates concerning the

---

12 Jean Laplanche, *Between Seduction and Inspiration: Man,* trans. Jeffrey Mehlman (New York: The Unconscious in Translation, 2015)

13 Sigmund Freud, "Analysis Terminable and Interminable," in *SE* 23:248.

14 Jean Laplanche, "Defence and Prohibition in Treatment and in the Psychoanalytic Account of the Human," trans. Luke Thurston, in *The Unfinished Copernican Revolution* (New York: The Unconscious in Translation, 2020), 41-56.

discovery of the analytic method on the one hand and, on the other, on the position of psychoanalysis within the human sciences. These postulates can be summarized as follows:

1) Like "all philosophy [psychoanalysis] must be anthropological: this does not imply a relativism but rather leads us to define universal categories of being human and becoming human."[15]

2) From this point of view, the object of psychoanalysis is part of these universal categories of becoming human and exists independently of psychoanalysis.

3) If analytic work is able to modify forces present in psychic conflict, the relations of force between the sexual unconscious and other components of the soul, this is because it recreates a "fundamental anthropological situation" that is at the origin of this sexual unconscious.

4) Psychoanalytic theory, metapsychology, and the invention of psychoanalytic treatment are indissociably linked.

It is well known that the discovery of psychoanalysis was first of all the discovery of a psychotherapeutic method derived from the cathartic method. But Laplanche's thinking about the origin of psychoanalysis goes far beyond that. He holds that in Freud's work not only does treatment have priority over metapsychology but also the discovery of the analytic method went hand in hand with

---

15 Jean Laplanche, "Temporality and Translation," trans. Luke Thurston, in *The Unfinished Copernican Revolution*, op. cit.), 401-422.

the theory of seduction.[16] This finding implies that the elaboration of psychoanalytic theory took place alongside observation of the group of phenomena at play in clinical psychoanalysis and particularly those that were left out of the thinking about the mode of action of hypnotherapy: the relationship between patient and therapist, including importantly the loving connection Freud later called "transference love."[17]

We will return to the notion of seduction that constitutes the heart of Laplanche's theory, a theory known as the general theory of seduction (GTS), but for now, we will emphasize the fact that, by underlining the simultaneity of the discovery of the analytic situation and Freud's elaboration of the theory of seduction Laplanche stresses a connection between Freud's grasping the therapeutic situation in its totality and his elaboration of a theory. Freud was able to grasp the link between the therapeutic situation with all its determinants—a totality including previously ignored factors essential to its effectiveness—and the elaboration of the theory of seduction. It was this link that led to the transformation of the therapeutic situation, allowing the invention of psychoanalytic practice. In focusing on this connection, Laplanche's analysis situates itself in the frame of dialectics and of rationalism: Transformation becomes possible at the moment when the capacity to grasp a situation completely, which is to say, concretely, brings together theory and practice.

The same derivation is found in the relationship Laplanche establishes between theory and practice in psychoanalysis, notably in his definition of the fundamental anthropological situation. According to him, metapsychology must be able to account not

16 Jean Laplanche, "Goals of the Psychoanalytic Process," in *Between Seduction and Inspiration: Man*, trans. Jeffrey Mehlman (New York: Unconscious in Translation, 2015), 189.

17 Sigmund Freud, "Observations on Transference-Love," in *SE* 12.

only for the life of the soul and its determinants but also for the action of psychoanalytic treatment. Therefore, the description of the origin of the sexual unconscious must include elements that can explain the work of reopening brought about by analysis, the term "analysis" being taken in its etymological sense of unbinding, unlinking. What is subject to unbinding? How do we explain the links that need to be unbound? What relationship is there between these bonds and the thoughts and passions that shape human behavior? And from the opposite angle, if in some circumstances psychoanalysis can facilitate unbinding, how does that further our understanding of the binding?

These questions are also part of the rationalist tradition. The connections between psychoanalysis as a theory of the human soul and clinical psychoanalysis are of the same nature as the connections between the unconscious and the human sciences. In both cases, there is a link between theory and practice. Both entail the capacity to grasp human relationships in their totality — in their concrete reality. Both derive from the principle that the unconscious is at work in all human activities, including thinking and emotional relations. Thus, the unconscious is at work in clinical analysis, just as it is in work relationships, in philosophical reflection, in legal theories, in one's relationship to the body, in everyday life, love, artistic creation, and sports. The link between the unconscious and human actions and emotions is not created by thought; it exists in reality. This is why, in Laplanche's theory, the description of the nature of the unconscious must also be able to account for specific aspects of the analytic cure and of what, in other favorable circumstances, gives us access to derivatives of the unconscious.

The analytic situation implies the simultaneous presence of two people. Laplanche makes this requirement also the foundation of his metapsychological theory of the formation of the sexual unconscious. Nevertheless, it is not a relational theory. His theory entails a redefinition of the main concepts of psychoanalysis in light of an epistemology anchored in the rationalist tradition. The titles of three of his works evoke the principal features of this tradition.

2. The Unfinished Copernican Revolution

The Unfinished Copernican Revolution (2019 [1992]), *The Temptation of Biology* (2011 [1993]), and *Life and Death in Psychoanalysis* (1970) are three titles that summarize the principal epistemological orientations of Laplanche's theory, orientations whose affiliation with the rationalist tradition can be shown. In this chapter, we will examine the thinking about the rationalist tradition provoked by the latter two titles. As for the Copernican revolution, we will tackle that in the next chapter by describing the general theory of seduction (GTS).

a) Life and Death in Psychoanalysis

While I do not intend to summarize *Life and Death in Psychoanalysis*, or to underline the modifications Laplanche's theory has undergone since this early work, it is useful to linger on the book's title, which allows us to locate the border that, in Laplanche's work, delimits the epistemological field of psychoanalysis. The word "psychoanalysis" means analysis of the soul. Laplanche's theory remains close to this definition: He defines and studies the concepts of psychoanalysis as phenomena of the soul, as phenomena that originate in the soul and that can be described as such. This does not imply that psychoanalytic treatment can have as its objective and effect only promotion of symbolization and expansion of the possibilities of psychical representation for the analysand by opening the way to feelings or affects that, though present as sensations before the treatment, did not present themselves as thoughts or even as thinkable. However, it does imply that the fundamental concepts of psychoanalysis—drive, sexual unconscious (sexuality in the psychoanalytic sense),[18] and ego—are defined as phenomena of the soul. What is a phenomenon of the soul? This expression covers thoughts, ideas, images, representations, fantasies, emotions, and feelings, to the extent that these assume a mental form, the form in which they present themselves to the soul, more precisely to the human soul.

In 1915, in additions to *Three Essays on the Theory of Sexuality* of 1905, Freud introduced the concepts of "drive representative" (*Triebrepräsentant*) and "ideational representative" (*Vorstellungsrepräsentanz*) to designate "the elements through which the drive finds its psychical expression" and thereby becomes an object of study for psychoanalysis.[19] Nevertheless, in Freudian theory, the drive constitutes a limit concept, at the border of the psychic and the somatic: Its source is in the body. This is why, beginning in 1915, Freud defines the drive as the demand for work that the body imposes on the soul. Laplanche reverses this definition. In his work the drives is not presented as a limit concept but as a phenomenon at the level of the psyche: It is the demand for work that the soul imposes on the body. More precisely: "The drive is therefore neither a mythical entity, nor a biological force, nor a concept on the frontier between the mental and the physical. It is the impact on the individual and the ego of the constant stimulation exerted from the inside by the repressed thing-representations, which can be described as source-objects of the drive."[20] In other words, "by inverting Freud's famous formulation, one can consider

---

18 Which Laplanche also calls "sexuality enlarged in the Freudian sense."

19 See Jean Laplanche and Jean-Bertrand Pontalis, *The Language of Psychoanalysis* (1973 [1967]).

20 Jean Laplanche, "The Drive and Its Source-Object," trans. Luke Thurston, in *The Unfinished Copernican Revolution*, op. cit. 293-311.

the drive to correspond to the 'demand for work' imposed on the body by its relation to repressed unconscious signifiers."[21]

Laplanche's definition implies two postulates: (1) The formation of the sexual unconscious is a consequence of repression, and (2) the drive comes from the unconscious, not the other way around. The first element implies that the unconscious is neither innate nor hereditary, that repression by the individual occurs prior to the formation of the sexual unconscious. The second excludes the possibility of a biological source for the drive. This definition is based on Freud's first theories, theories from which he distanced himself as he increasingly moved toward a more hereditary conception of the unconscious. Laplanche writes: "To state things formulaically, I might say that at one stage in Freud's thinking the unconscious will arise from the drive, then the drive from the somatic, but that before 1897 it is the drive that arises from the unconscious."[22]

How does Laplanche's definition relate to the rationalist tradition? There are three essential points: (1) the description of the object of psychoanalysis in its concrete manifestations, (2) the epistemological divisions that situate the contributions of psychoanalysis in relation to understanding the phenomena of the soul, and (3) the refusal of a leap into irrationality to explain the passage from the somatic to the mental and from the social to the individual.

A Nonspeculative Description of the Domain of Psychoanalysis

Laplanche's position, according to which the unconscious, the drive,

21 Jean Laplanche, "Three Meanings of the Term 'Unconscious,'" in *Freud and the Sexual* (New York: Unconscious in Translation, 2011), 209.

22 Jean Laplanche, "The Unfinished Copernican Revolution," in *The Unfinished Copernican Revolution* trans. Luke Thurston, op. cit. 3-40.

and the ego are phenomena and categories of the soul, permits us to identify what these concepts, these mental agencies, represent concretely. Thus, for instance, the sexual unconscious, which begets the drive, is made up of fragments of scenes, of representations, and of fantasms or, more precisely, of fantasies.[23] Such a description does not make the contents less real. On the contrary, they have a reality of their own and are essential components of reason, will, and the emotions. They work on the body and shape actions and decisions. The unconscious is not a metaphysical entity. It corresponds to the particular contents, highly specific to each individual, that, in the form of fantasy and the excitation it provokes, constitute the object of study of psychoanalysis: "Fantasy, in its originary link to excitation," constitutes "the genuine, nonspeculative domain of psychoanalysis."[24] This constitutes the mental form of human sexuality. It works on the body; affects health; is inseparable from subjectivity, cognitive functioning, and affective states; and, on this basis, takes part in social relations.

The Delimitation of Psychoanalysis's Epistemological Field

It does not follow that all human sciences must include psychoanalysis in their field of study. Nor does psychoanalysis include the study of biological, psychological, sociological, or political aspects of the human condition, which is not to say that these have no impact on the soul or that psychoanalysis can ignore them. No discipline should suggest that the part of reality

---

23 *Le Vocabulaire de la psychanalyse* has no entry on fantasy [*fantaisie*] but only on phantasy [*fantasm*]. In his subsequent writings, Laplanche uses the term fantasy (*fantaisie*) to designate the contents of the sexual unconscious. For Laplanche, phantasy [*fantasm*] is a more general expression that also covers daydreams and similarly coherent scenarios in which, of course, unconscious fantasy is also at work.

24 Jean Laplanche, "Masochism and the General Theory of Seduction," trans. Luke Thurston, in *The Unfinished Copernican Revolution* op. cit., 541-561

it illuminates is in any sense the whole of reality. The rationalist perspective requires that we maintain the perspective of a whole, of a complete and therefore concrete reality; an abstraction is precisely the illusion that one or several partial elements of reality can by themselves provide a full and fair representation of a reality. The possibility of accounting in thought for reality in its concrete dimension—since an abstract reality is not a reality but an idea— requires each discipline to delimit its epistemological field in order to reveal, from the perspective of a totality, the coherent and dynamic aspect of its particular contribution.

Laplanche's theory is based on requiring reaffirmation the epistemological field proper to psychoanalysis while acknowledging the legitimacy of other domains of research. The border of this field depends, at the same time, on the specification and the definition of the object of psychoanalysis. As we have said, the object of psychoanalysis is the unconscious and the ways of accessing it, while fantasy is its domain of investigation and its angle of intervention. Thus, we are dealing with mental processes affecting the body and acting in the affective sphere, in intellectual life, and in relational life. Psychoanalysis's epistemological domain is not delimited by the opposition of body and soul or of affect and rationality or of individual and society, but rather by tracing the line that separates sexuality and self-preservation.[25] The border of the field is located at the point where sexuality takes over the functions of self-preservation and the sphere of the needs, investing them with an energy driven by a completely different logic. In fact, the field where psychoanalysis exists is no more marked by the soul/body opposition than by the separation between rationality on the one hand and the irrational or emotional on the other. As

---

25 Laplanche, "Three Meanings of the Term 'Unconscious,'" in *Freud and The Sexual*, (New York: The Unconscious In Translation, 2011 [2007]). page 210n7.

Laplanche writes, "Psychoanalysis is no more and no less closely related to neurobiological processes than is aesthetics, say, or logic or the reasoning of the physicist. The fact is that the order of thought forms a whole, just as the material order does. There is no mental process of which it may be said that it is more dependent than some other one on its material underpinning."[26]

The Refusal of a Leap into the Irrational

The epistemological divisions described by Laplanche avoid a pitfall many disciplines encounter when they give an account of the link between body and soul and/or of the passage from the social to the individual.

—Matter and Thought

The attribution of an endogenous, biological source to the unconscious raises an important question: How does a bodily (or material) process—including a somatic excitation—become a thought process? In psychoanalysis the question might be phrased: How does a drive arising from the body take on the form of fantasy? This question often elicits unsatisfying responses, responses that mostly skirt the problem, particularly from the perspective of rationalism.

Let's examine the parameters of this problem more closely. The materialist thesis that matter is the source of all reality is problematic when it comes to accounting for the content of thoughts. This thesis is, in one form or other, widespread enough today in psychoanalysis, especially in theorizing that brings together psychoanalysis and the neurosciences. The thesis also serves as an argument against psychoanalysis if it is presumed

---

26 Jean Laplanche, *The Temptation of Biology*, trans. Donald Nicholson-Smith (New York: Unconscious in Translation, 2015 [1993]), 117.

to mean that the discoveries of biology or pharmacology render psychoanalysis obsolete. But fantasy involves thought processes: Even if it has a material base, it also has content, a content that is precisely the object of psychoanalytic attention. As Laplanche writes, "If, miraculously, biological research ever managed to account for every thought process in physical terms, the biologist would have no further questions to answer. His interlocutors would be convinced by purely material means. This speculation plunges us, however, into an abysmal perplexity: Are we to suppose, say, that one day the content of an article in a neuroscientific journal could be injected like a neuroleptic drug?"[27]

Freudian theory poses a similar problem when it holds that drive with a somatic origin is the source of the sexual unconscious: namely, how to account for the sexual character of the drive. In other words, how to account for its fantasmatic form if its source is a somatic excitation? Furthermore, how should we explain the transformation of a pressure whose origin is somatic into fantasy? Or, how should we account for the link between this pressure and its psychical representatives? One possible response is to avoid the question by referring to a sort of psychical creativity, which would not be much more than nominalism and, in the words of Laplanche, would lead back "to the fiction of hallucinatory satisfaction (of need? of desire?)—which is still too often considered to be beyond criticism."[28]

One way of getting around the problem of the fantasmatic content of the drive is to postulate the existence of universal, primal fantasies transmitted by heredity. We find this type of

---

27 Jean Laplanche, "Biologism and Biology," in *The Temptation of Biology: Freud's Theories of Sexuality*, op. cit., 116

28 Jean Laplanche, "Sexuality and Attachment," in *Freud and the Sexual*, 49. 29 F. A. Yates, *Giordano Bruno and the Hermetic Tradition*,(Chicago: University of Chicago Press, 1964).

reasoning in Freud's phylogenetic theory—primal fantasies at the source of psychoanalysis's great complexes such as Oedipus and castration. The connection with irrationalism is manifest in the idea that there is a relationship between the individual soul and universal, immemorial contents. Although this formulation does not correspond exactly to the supposed mode of transmission of primal fantasies, it is necessary to underline the commonalities this theory shares with the principles of hermeticism and magic, principles according to which an omniscient universal soul would maintain a relationship with certain regions of the individual soul.[29]

[29]The epistemological division described by Laplanche does not imply the passage from the somatic either to the psychical or to primal fantasies; it posits that the infant's sexuality—in other words, unconscious fantasy—comes from material that is already sexual and fantasmatic: the sexual fantasies of the adult caregivers. These fantasies already belong to the mental order—they are not somatic—and they are already sexual. They are transmitted to the infant by way of interhuman communication: verbal and nonverbal messages addressed to the infant.[30]

Communication is not a specifically human phenomenon. Nevertheless, interhuman communication has its source in a context that is specifically human. This context corresponds to what Laplanche calls "the fundamental anthropological situation," which is characterized by the simultaneous presence of an adult who has a sexual unconscious and a child who does not yet have one. The adult's sexual unconscious infiltrates—compromises in the psychoanalytic sense of "compromise"—the messages of the care and tenderness addressed to the infant. In this way the adult's

---

29 F. A. Yates, Giordano Bruno and the Hermetic Tradition,(Chicago: University of Chicago Press, 1964).

30 Laplanche, "Three Meanings of the Term 'Unconscious,'" op. cit. 204.

fantasy becomes implanted in the "psychophysiological skin" of the infant.

Here a clarification is necessary. Emphasizing that Laplanche's theory is a theory of the soul is not meant to obscure or minimize the importance of the infant's body in that theory. To the contrary, the epistemological distinction between sexuality and self-preservation—which is not the same as the distinction between body and soul—takes for granted the existence of a living body possessing the characteristics and properties necessary for its development as a human organism. Laplanche's theory is not a theological theory; it does not postulate the existence of a soul independent of the body. For the adult's message to be implanted in the body of the infant, an "initial somatic receptivity" is taken as a given. Nevertheless, as Laplanche specifies, this initial excitability is not sexual in the Freudian sense: "A general organic excitability must certainly be preexistent, but something else is needed in order to make it a drive."[31] Metapsychology is concerned precisely with the link that is formed between fantasy and excitation. This "something else" is the adult's fantasy and its content's link, already present in the adult, to excitation.

When we delineate the theory of generalized seduction, we will see how the adult's fantasy is not to be found as such in the infant but how, rather, the infant elaborates its own fantasies in a singular way. For the moment, we will focus on the rationalist aspects of Laplanche's theory, which are embodied in its critique of "creativist" and "illusionist" conceptions of human sexuality according to which the self-preservative activity would be transformed into fantasies: "If the sexual is not present *within* the original, *real experience*, it will never be rediscovered in the fantasmatic reproduction or the

---

31 Laplanche, "Sexuality and Attachment," in *Freud and the Sexual,* op. cit. 48.

symbolic elaboration of that experience."[32]

This critique involves questioning the theory of leaning-on that was an earlier theory of Laplanche, a theory he later rejected because it required a leap into the irrational, even into magic. As he writes:

> If infantile sexuality does not have an innate endog-
> enous mechanism, how can it emerge conjointly
> with self-preservation? And if it corresponds to
> a simple representation in fantasy of bodily at-
> tachment and self-preservative functions, by what
> miracle would this fantasmatization alone confer
> a sexual character upon somatic functions? As I
> have pointed out on several occasions, in Freud
> the putative "experience of satisfaction" and the
> putative "hallucinatory satisfaction of desire" are
> successful exercises in prestidigitation. They make
> the sexual emerge from the lack of satisfaction of
> the selfpreservative instinct in the same way that
> that rabbit emerges from the magician's hat. But
> the trick depends precisely on the fact that there is
> someone who has put the rabbit in the hat—and it
> is certainly the adult who put it there. [33]

—The Passage from the Collective to the Individual and from the Individual to the Collective

Psychoanalysis cannot ignore the fact that humans live in sociohistorical and cultural conditions that shape and are shaped by their thoughts and actions. Therefore, psychoanalysis must consider the interface between the forces arising from the sexual

32 Ibid., 46.

33 Jean Laplanche, "Drive and Instinct," in *Freud and the Sexual*, 20–21.

unconscious and the social conditions that define the individual. The GTS provides a framework for reflecting on relations between the social and the individual. This does not avoid the problems posed by the passage from external to internal and does not call into question the essentially social character of subjectivity.

In his theorizing, Laplanche did not explicitly develop the aspect of sociohistorical and cultural conditions shaping and shaped by individuals alone and in groups. His theory is not primarily concerned with subjectivity—a philosophical and psychological notion whose history is linked with theology—but with the constitution of the unconscious and with the agencies of the soul. The theory intervenes after these psychic agencies are constituted and is not reducible to them. Neither the unconscious nor the ego corresponds to subjectivity or to the "self,"[34] even if contemporary psychoanalysis—in particular the relational current—establishes a near equivalence between *"self"* and subjectivity.

The GTS posits that the constitution of the sexual unconscious is at the origin of the process of the infant's humanization: sexuality—enlarged sexuality, in the sense we have defined it—is a "condition of becoming human."[35] It marks the passage from a living being to a living human being.[36] For this reason, repression and the constitution of unconscious sexuality are preconditions for formation of subjectivity.

This point is essential to understanding Laplanche's anthropology and to situating it in relation to rationalism. Laplanche offers an essentially social analysis of the constitution

---

34 In the psychoanalytic sense, as a function of the ego or as the irrational part of the ego. The philosophical definition of self, especially in Locke, has closer links with subjectivity. A. De Libera, *Archéologie du sujet*, vol. 1, *Naissance du sujet* (Paris: Vrin, 2007).

35 Laplanche, "Temporality and Translation," 418-419.

36 Laplanche, *The Temptation of Biology.*

of the psychical agencies and, as a corollary, of the constitution of subjectivity. In the last analysis, the GTS implies that subjectivity cannot exist without sexualization and that sexualization comes from the fantasy of another person, an adult human, transmitted in a situation of communication. Consequently, sexualization is humanization and depends on the intervention of a subject who is already human and thus already sexualized. This is why Laplanche does not endorse the phenomenological position according to which the flesh would immediately be constitutive of subjectivity. In effect, he critiques Husserl and Merleau-Ponty for "reintroducing the human being with his 'flesh,' his native 'soil,' in a word, the earth itself as his primal habitat, the 'ark' he shares with the animals, into the 'constitutive ego.'"[37]

The GTS excludes any reference to an individual or a universal human nature that preexists what must be called social shaping or conditioning. From this point of view, psychoanalysis can extricate itself from a mythical use of anatomy, as well as from the naturalism of sexual stereotypes and from gendered relations of domination. This step is essential if psychoanalysis is to have the ability to contribute to a critical reflection on society without leading other disciplines down normative paths that scientifically are utterly suspect. In the GTS, sexualization, a prerequisite for subjectivity, has its source in the relationship of the nursling with the adult human who, by definition, is already sexualized, which is to say, who already has a sexual unconscious. Sexualization is not sexuation.[38] Here "adult" does not designate a parent of a specific sex, nor even a member of the infant's family. The term "adult"

---

37 Laplanche, "Unfinished Copernican Revolution," op. cit.

38 Laplanche writes: "My position implies distinguishing between the terms "sexualizing" [= linking to sexuality] and "sexing" [= linking to sexual difference]. Jean Laplanche, "Trauma, Translation, Transference and Other Trans(es)" in *The Unfinished Copernican Revolution* op. cit. 327-349

refers to any adult—or older child—who takes care of the infant. This is also why, in the GTS, no reference is made to the "feminine" or the "masculine," or to "psychical bisexuality," or to so-called maternal or paternal "functions," notions used abundantly in contemporary psychoanalysis.

In the GTS, the formation of the sexual unconscious and of the ego are simultaneous and are the result of primal repression. Here, it may be useful to point that Laplanche uses the term "originary" ['originaire' which is often translated as 'primal' e.g. in the Standard Edition.] He writes: "I reserve the qualification "originary" to designate a phenomenon which is not only first, or fundamental, or "primary" but which is essential to the origin of the field in which the phenomenon itself is defined. What is "before" this "origin" usually appears as a myth which contains, retroactively projected, some major features of what will come "afterwards."[39] Originary repression itself is a result of enigmatic messages coming from the other human.[40] At this point, without a detailed exposition of the theory, let me simply stress the following sequence. The message of the other is at the source of repression, which is itself constitutive of the "apparatus of the soul": the ego and the unconscious. Thus, in this theory, neither the ego nor the unconscious is cut off from their source in the social. The sexual unconscious makes itself known through its derivatives in the form of fragments of scenarios and of images that may later acquire a more "bound" aspect, which is to say, be given meaning. The contents of these fragments and the source of their meaning do not come from nowhere. They have their origin in a message that is itself bound, which is to say that a message has acquired meaning based on its origin in what has meaning in a given society. In addition, the ego can translate the

---

39 Laplanche, "Unfinished Copernican Revolution," op. cit.

40 These concepts will be explained in the next chapter.

messages thanks to "codes of translation" that are furnished by society as they are filtered through those who surround the infant. Such codes are meaningful only within a specific sociohistorical context. The modes of binding fragments and of translating messages cannot be the same for the child of a medieval serf as for the child of a family of socialist intellectuals in the twentyfirst century. In this way, the content of the fragments of images and later of fantasies, while peculiar to each individual, depend not only of the individual's history but also on the scenarios and codes offered by the individual's milieu and by the broader culture. Thus, although the unconscious and the ego are specific to each individual, strictly speaking, neither is "subjective," the former because its origin comes directly from another, the latter because it is at first constructed in the context of codes coming from the outside.

We have shown that the GTS offers a perspective on the relationships between subjectivity and society that does not invoke the concept of internalization. It is a concept of dubious value[41] that presupposes an original or "natural" subjectivity—not socially constructed but having the function of "internalizing" social contents. Moreover, internalization only names a process without explaining what the process is and without giving an account of how it works. How does internalization happen? By what path would external content become internal content? From these two points of view, internalization entails an irrational position on the relationship between the collective and the individual.

Laplanche's theory enriches sociological conceptions by taking account of sexualization—in other words, of fantasy. It introduces the dimension of libidinal investment into the consideration of

---

41 See, e.g., Christophe Dejours in A. Green et al., *Sur la théorie de la séduction* (Paris: Libres Cahiers pour la psychanalyse, 2003), 55–69.

human thoughts and actions, a dimension essential to a concrete description. In this way, the GTS modifies the conception of collective relationships. In the tradition of rationalist thought, the description of sexualization as a process of humanization implies the rejection of any endogenous or hereditary transmission of the sexual unconscious, whatever form the unconscious takes. This is why Laplanche persistently denounces the various manifestations of the "biological temptation," the biologizing of human sexuality, characteristic of contemporary psychoanalysis.

b) The Misguided Biologizing of Sexuality

The rationalist features of the GTS largely stem from the following postulates:

1. The child's sexuality must arise from material that is already sexual;
2. This material can be found only in those who care for the infant;
3. The simultaneous presence of an adult—or older child— who possesses a sexual unconscious and an infant who does not yet have one constitutes a universal and fundamental anthropological situation that gives rise to originary primal repression and to the constitution of the sexual unconscious

These three elements are incompatible with theories that attribute an endogenous or hereditary source to the unconscious,[42] notably by identifying something within the unconscious that preexists repression by the individual. On this point, Laplanche

42 In "Three Meanings of the Term 'Unconscious,'" Laplanche also identifies a nonrepressed unconscious, "the unconscious enclave"; it is a nonsexual unconscious whose source is also in the adult's message. It is not a biological or hereditary unconscious that existed before primal repression and from which the sexual unconscious would eventually emerge.

found himself as much in debate with Freud as with post-Freudian theorizing. In fact, Laplanche critiqued the diverse forms, including those adopted by Freud, of the hypothesis that there is a biological or a hereditary source for the unconscious or for its contents, grouping them under the rubric of "the genetic lineage." Instead of correctly giving "preponderance to the process of repression, and thus to a creation of the unconscious during each individual's existence, there is a constant temptation to situate the unconscious in one or another genetic lineage in which it would occupy a position of a first (or primordial) element."[43]

The Genetic Lineage in Psychoanalysis

What Laplanche calls the genetic lineage appears in four forms. First, there is the psychological form, according to which "all that is conscious was first unconscious." According to this version, the unconscious would correspond to the mind's primitive processes, from which consciousness would emerge. Thus, in the beginning, the unconscious is not repressed; repression intervenes in a secondary manner as a mechanism of defense. This form of the genetic lineage is essentially a reference to Hartmann's *ego-psychology*, which, through its effort to turn psychoanalysis into a general psychology, cleared the path for the contemporary relational schools. Today, the psychological line can be found in metapsychology that combines psychoanalysis and the cognitive sciences in the definition of the unconscious.[44] It also has a significant influence on the intersubjectivist orientations, for which the term "unconscious" is only descriptive and designates that of which we are unaware.[45]

---

43 Jean Laplanche, "A Brief Treatise on the Unconscious," in *Between Seduction and Inspiration: Man*, op. cit. 58.

44 For example, some of the positions of Peter Fonagy.

45 Tessier, *La psychanalyse américaine*, and Tessier, "Jean Laplanche in Rational

The second version of the genetic lineage takes a form that relies on individual biology. According to this theory, the id makes up the unrepressed part of the unconscious and is the great reservoir of the drives; it opens directly onto the body. This hypothesis is at the foundation of the Kleinian orientation, for which the "death instinct" exists from the beginning. Not only the id but also the ego — in other words "the apparatus of the soul" in the psychoanalytic sense of the term — is present from the beginning. Consequently, in this view, repression is not necessary for formation of the human soul. Instead the soul has its source in biological functions.

The third version of a genetic lineage invokes phylogenesis; primal fantasies are presumed to form the kernel of the unconscious. This line of thinking is particularly important in French psychoanalysis, as well as, in a general way, in classical psychoanalysis. Primal fantasies correspond to the major complexes of psychoanalysis, notably Oedipus, castration, and the primal scene. The phylogenetic form of the genetic lineage does not present the hypothesis of an unconscious that is there from the beginning but rather recognizes the necessity of repression for its formation. Nevertheless, the contents of the unconscious are considered to be universal, predetermined, and hereditary — independent of individual history.

The fourth instantiation of the genetic lineage is found in Freud's "metabiological and metacosmologic thought" thought in *Beyond the Pleasure Principle*, in which "the unconscious is assimilated to a primordial id."[46] In this line of thinking, which corresponds to Freud's second dualism of the drives — the Eros/Thanatos opposition — the sexual unconscious is not produced by repression. We should note

---

Perspective: Translation as a Basic Anthropological Situation in Psychoanalysis," *Revue canadienne de psychanalyse* 18, no. 2 (2010): 281–329.

46 Laplanche, "A Brief Treatise on the Unconscious," op. cit. p. 59.

that Laplanche, who has systematically critiqued the notion of the death drive as a metabiological speculation, nevertheless does not reject the idea of a sexual death drive corresponding to the most unbound aspects of sexual drive.

Epistemological Questions in Contemporary Psychoanalysis

For the most part, contemporary psychoanalytic orientations adopt a genetic lineage for the unconscious. In this respect, the GTS is profoundly different, notably because of its consistent adherence to the rationalist tradition—at least that is the thesis of this book. Moreover, even though contemporary psychoanalysis is still sometimes presented as a unified discipline, it is made up of a great variety of theories—often mutually incompatible. Indeed, it is now diversified to the point that it is difficult to argue that such concepts as unconscious, drive, sexuality, and even psychoanalysis itself refer to a shared reality. And yet, outside of psychoanalytic circles, the term "psychoanalysis" is presumed to evoke a relatively precise reality. In popular culture, it usually refers to a form of psychology centered on the primacy of childhood, colored by a certain normativity structured by sexual difference and concepts linked to phylogenesis, such as the Oedipus complex. These two facts create difficulties, particularly for the relationship between psychoanalysis and other disciplines.

Within the psychoanalytic community, we cultivate the illusion of a shared language, in which the most divergent definitions coexist even though they describe incompatible views of reality. It has become a major obstacle to the contributions that psychoanalysis could make to clinical and social fields. This false facade also prevents any substantive epistemological critique of psychoanalysis. The divergences are never genuinely taken up as such, and the radical incompatibility of some positions is systematically concealed.

Under these conditions, some psychoanalysts permit themselves to entertain the idea that it is unnecessary to make a choice among the various theories, that it is useless to take a position in favor of one theoretical option over another.

To locate Laplanche's theory in the frame of contemporary epistemological theories, it will be helpful to define the conception of the sexual unconscious that one finds in what are currently the most influential orientations. As we are locating these definitions on a philosophical level, the goal is not to bring out their nuances but, on the contrary, to group them based on their commonalities. Two main trends can be seen. There are some Anglo-Saxon currents in which the relational orientation has become very important. With the term "relational orientation," we are pointing to those schools of thought in which the unconscious represents a subjective psychical reality arising from early relational schemata that the clinical analysis seeks to understand. Such metapsychology belongs to both the psychological and the biological lineages described by Laplanche. In contrast, we find the traditional or classical trends, considered to be more Freudian, which remain close to the phylogenetic lineage.[47] The traditional trend, in the sense that we are using the term, groups together theories in which the unconscious and the drive are, in important respects, defined by reference to sexual difference and/or to primal fantasies and/or to mytho-symbolic entities. The relational and traditional tendencies, which will be described more precisely in the pages that follow, are not mutually exclusive. In contemporary psychoanalysis, theoretical allegiances no longer require strict theoretical positions. Thus, we find references to Oedipus,[48] to castration, and to Freud's

---

47 This includes Lacanian orientations, although one hesitates to call them traditional.

48 For instance, one finds the notions of the "oedipal" and the "preoedipal" child in the intersubjectivist orientation.

anthropology in the relational theorists. Similarly, representatives of traditional theory often refer to relational theory. It needs to be said that this was not always the case.

The expression "Anglo-Saxon currents" is used here in a general way to bring together the British and American object-relations schools in their present versions with some intersubjectivist thinking and with the social-constructionist theories—the latter have been very critical of classical American psychoanalysis and Freudian anthropology.[49] In other words, since we are focusing on the definition of the sexual unconscious, we are putting together those contemporary theories that the traditional theories criticize, or have criticized, for desexualizing psychoanalysis, for in some way sanitizing it. Here this critique must be examined closely. In fact, Laplanche makes a similar critique of traditional metapsychology itself. For Laplanche, centering the human subject on its biological origin and on its intimate and unknown personal psychology or focusing on primal fantasies that appear as transmitted intergenerationally and already bound are both ways of sweeping aside the polymorphous, perverse, and unbound aspects of infantile sexuality and thus, at the same time, the demonic alterity of sexuality in the human soul. The next step is to show that the two modes of centering the human subject characteristic of Anglo-Saxon currents and of traditional metapsychology are two forms of irrationalism each of which is tied to romanticism: for one mode, this involves the defense of psychological subjectivity and the subjectivism of knowledge, for the other the emphasis is on the theory of the mytho-symbolic.

—The Anglo-Saxon Orientations

Contemporary trends in Anglo-Saxon theorizing emphasize

49 For example, Roy Schafer, Donald Spence. See Tessier, *La psychanalyse américaine*.

subjectivity and the intersubjective relationship that characterizes both the analytic relation and the formation of psychic life. What's more, the term "object relation" typically refers to a subject/object relationship in which the subject constructs its object, in large part through projection. Despite the primacy they attribute to the earliest relationships, these theories are profoundly different from Laplanche's theory, which is not concerned with the relationship between two subjects but with the formation of the child's sexual unconscious starting from the adult's unconscious in the primal, asymmetric context of the adult/ child situation. The asymmetry in question is not the asymmetry due to the infant's dependency—though that is incontestable—but the asymmetry established by the fact that the child, who does not yet have a sexual unconscious, is in the presence of an adult whose sexual unconscious exists and acts. Furthermore, in contemporary AngloSaxon orientations, the sexuality/self-preservation dualism has been replaced by opposition between love and hate, an opposition in which metapsychology has little place. The *self*, which in Freudian theory corresponds to a function of the ego,[50] takes the place of the structural agencies. In such theories, the unconscious refers in a general way to the affects, affects that are unknown, diverted from their primary destination, repressed, or buried in the deepest part of the *self*.

Contemporary Anglo-Saxon theorizing has many philosophical sources. Thus, the socioconstructionist schools, which contested the interpretive canons of traditional psychoanalysis, their phylogenetic symbolism, and their reification of metapsychological concepts, are principally tied to phenomenology.[51] They emphasize the intentionality of psychical acts and the role of the interpreter in the

---

50 Its identifying or irrational aspect.

51 Roy Schafer was an important representative.

construction of meaning.[52] Recently their views have become more eclectic. They insist on intersubjectivity as the necessary condition for the birth of the subject. Here there is a notion, also evocative of phenomenology, according to which the "we" precedes the "me." This conception is problematic for psychoanalysis. For one thing, the term "intersubjective" presupposes the simultaneous presence of two subjects—although the notion of the subject is precisely what psychoanalysis has helped to shatter. In addition, this conception does not allow questions about the provenance of the two subjects who constitute the first intersubjectivity. The relational theories readily attribute an origin to the first subjectivity grounded in the biological or the neuropsychological, an origin outside of the domain of psychoanalysis.

Furthermore, beyond referring to the early relations of the nursling, the Anglo-Saxon schools emphasize the intersubjective relation that is the analytic relation, as well as the emotional experience of the session and the elaboration of the meaning of this experience. Therefore, they pay close attention to the sensations and feelings of the participants, as well as to the preponderant role played by subjectivity, essentially defined as psychological subjectivity, both the source of knowledge and a tool for narrative creation. Interpretation itself represents an interpersonal communication that provides a new opportunity for emotional contacts that are supposed to promote a richer narrative. Thus, interpretation constitutes a hermeneutic activity based not on a preexisting symbolism but on the integration of subjective feelings in a process of auto-theorization and auto-historicization. Although I do not question its therapeutic potential,[53] it is difficult to reconcile

---

52 Tessier, *La pscyhanalyse américaine.*

53 Laplanche writes: "All psychoanalysis is devoted primarily to psychotherapy: to the self-narration of the subject with the more or less active assistance of the analyst." "Psychoanalysis and Psychotherapy," in *Freud and the Sexual*, 282.

such a perspective with the conception of a sexual unconscious that resists all communicative logic, in particular the logic of meaning and of signifying.

Contemporary intersubjectivist thinking finds it easy to accept the hypothesis of precocious psychological structures at the origin of psychic life, structures overdetermined by relational factors but bound in part to environmental factors and in part to constitutional factors, structures deemed to be inscribed in cerebral, anatomical, and physiological phenomena. Therefore, for the intersubjectivist, psychoanalysis shares a border with biology. This border, as well as the psychological conception of subjectivity and the importance given to projection as an instrument for apprehending the exterior world, contributes to turning psychoanalysis into a theory of knowledge in which the emphasis is placed on affective and projective elements in the creation of a subjective reality. In this way, psychoanalysis finds a connection with cognitive psychology and neurosciences, and accordingly these disciplines can explore paths of mutual validation.[54]

In terms of philosophical traditions, even if one can recognize the influence of transcendentalism and British romanticism in certain trends, Anglo-Saxon orientations remain, above all, marked by pragmatism, which exerted a decisive influence on American psychology at the beginning of the twentieth century.[55] On the one hand, the subjectivity to which Anglo-Saxon metapsychology refers corresponds to experience, conscious experience, in the tradition of William James's "stream of consciousness." On the other hand, it has functionalist aspects, which are themselves linked to pragmatism: consciousness functioning as knowledge and, in return, knowledge, insofar as it has a physical origin, becoming

---

54 The work of Wilma Bucci and especially of Peter Fonagy can be cited in this regard—see Tessier, *La psychanalyse américaine*.

55 Ibid.

an attribute of consciousness. Knowledge then has to be treated as a psychophysical phenomenon, and as a result, the theory of knowledge is no longer grounded in philosophy but instead must rely on psychology and neurophysiology. Thus, the critical aspect of the theory of knowledge is reduced to a more or less pertinent element.

Such naturalization of epistemology is characteristic of major trends among philosophies of mind that are tied to pragmatism, for example, the British analytic tradition. These philosophies have exerted a powerful influence in contemporary culture, including within psychoanalysis. While partially in continuity with behaviorism, these philosophies of mind have called into question behaviorism's exclusion of factors related to desire and to intentionality as determinants of behavior. Some philosophies of mind have brought these factors back into discussion and, indeed, consider them indispensable to a theory of mind.[56] This position shows the strong ties within AngloSaxon currents between psychoanalysis and the theory of knowledge on one hand and, on the other, the theory of knowledge and the theory of thought.[57] This is why the model of learning as a factor in therapeutic change occupies a central place in Anglo-Saxon psychoanalysis, especially learning in the affective sphere. The experience of new modes of relating promotes the development of a new network of beliefs and representations allowing patients to better understand their own behavior and the behavior of others (e.g., Fonagy).[58]

---

56 D. Fisette and P. Poirier, *Philosophie de l'esprit: Psychologie du sens commun et sciences de l'esprit* (Paris: Vrin, 2002).

57 Bion, for example, describes psychoanalysis as a theory of thought. Although his theory is not related to the philosophies of the mind, their influence allows us to better understand why the idea that psychoanalysis could constitute a theory of thought is easily accepted.

58 Fonagy, "Some Complexities in the Relationship of Psychoanalytic Theory to Technique."

There is a logical connection between the disinterest in the sexual unconscious, or at least disinterest in what Laplanche calls the "realism of the unconscious"—the unconscious as a distinct psychical reality—and the gnoseology that characterizes the clinical conceptions of the relational schools.[59] These conceptions emphasize the subjective character not only of lived experience but also of knowledge. In fact, they hold that individuals can know only the reality that they have themselves constructed or, more restrictively, that only the constructed real is meaningful and operational for the individual. From this perspective, these conceptions come close to subjective idealism, according to which there would exist no reality independent of our consciousness. Under these conditions, it is logical that, on the level of theory, the relational schools reject the hypothesis of an agency that, while not material, would have the reality of a thing and that, while outside of consciousness, would have an existence independent of consciousness.

We must recall that, in the American socioconstructionist schools, the refusal to refer to a sexual unconscious at first amounted to an epistemological critique of classical psychoanalysis, particularly of its notion of an unconscious constituted by drives arising from the major complexes. These schools did not accept that such complexes could serve as objective foundations for psychoanalytic interpretations. They challenged classical psychoanalysis's phallocentric and ethnocentric character. This tendency, while less discussed now than it was at the beginning, is still found in the American psychoanalysis. It is regrettable that the psychoanalysts who rejected the sexism inherent in the classic descriptions of a primal unconscious believed the same logic obligated them to

---

59 These are the dominant orientations in the contemporary eclecticism. Historically, there have been several distinctions to be made concerning, for example, the Kleinian theory, but the tendency is strong toward a psychoanalysis that is increasingly close to psychological psychotherapy.

reject the importance of sexuality in psychoanalysis. Moreover, in Anglo-Saxon psychoanalysis, many post-Freudian movements had already, for reasons that were not necessarily related to the Freudian theory of the drives, minimized the role of the sexual factor both in theory and in clinical work.

The culturalist and constructivist critique is not alone in its disinterest in the sexual unconscious. Winnicottian and neo-Winnicottian theories, powerfully influential in contemporary psychoanalysis, have contributed to this disinterest since they have gradually abandoned all reference to the drive. On some points, attachment theories are close to the relational orientations. They emphasize the psychological dimension of trauma related to pathological forms of attachment, as well as their neurobiological consequences. The drive is often considered an obsolete notion. Yet certain representatives of the relational schools, sensitive to criticism of the desexualization of psychoanalysis, wish to restore a reference to the sexual. It is disappointing to note that, in trying to reconnect with the "drive," some intersubjectivists assimilate sexuality to elements related to the primal scene, and to Oedipus, and to psychosexual stages, thus revealing the influence social representations tied to phylogenetic symbolism continue to have on their ideas.[60]

—The Traditional Orientation

The classical or traditional orientation is the other current arising from Freudian theory. It postulates the existence of a primal unconscious, made up of the universal fantasies that are the foundations of the major complexes of psychoanalysis such as Oedipus and castration. This orientation runs through the whole

---

60 Hélène Tessier. "Pulsion et subjectivité", *Libres Cahiers pour la psychanalyse*, n°
15, *La pulsion et le destin.*

of classical psychoanalysis. It has retained an importance in French psychoanalysis,[61] even though French psychoanalysis has become more and more integrated with Anglo-Saxon orientations, in particular that of Donald Woods Winnicott.[62]

Such traditional theorizing attaches much more importance to Freud's phylogenetic theory[6363] than does the Anglo-Saxon current. It assigns a major role to myth in the determination of the contents of the sexual unconscious. Those contemporary currents that are firmly linked to traditional metapsychology refer to Oedipus, castration, the murder of the father, and the primal scene without making clear their relationship to the theory of the drives. In the phylogenetic theory, the relationship between myth and the contents of the unconscious depends on the concept of representation and hereditary disposition as postulated by Freud to account for the content of the primal fantasies. Freudian theory identifies two types of internal mooring for the drive: a somatic one, in the form of erogenous zones and the stages of psychosexual development, and a genetic one, in the form of the original contents of the drive's representative-representation.[64]

---

61 Lacan's theory, strictly speaking not part of traditional psychoanalysis, has contributed to this current and, on the points relating to phylogenesis, exerts a significant influence, especially on applied psychoanalysis.

62 The traditional stream has also occupied a significant place in Anglo-Saxon psychoanalysis, although in different forms from those it has taken in French psychoanalysis. This was particularly the case in ego-psychology. It is still found in contemporary orientations but more and more associated with relational currents.

63 Grubrich-Simitis refers to the phylogenetic fantasy of Freud. However, the reference to phylogenesis can be found at several points in the elaboration of Freud's thought and constitutes a significant aspect of certain aspects of his metapsychology. 64 I. Grubrich-Simitis, "Zum Verhältnis von Trauma und Trieb," *Psyche* 41 (1987): 992–1023; I. Grubrich-Simitis "Trauma oder Trieb—Trieb und Trauma: Wiederbetrachtet," *Psyche* 7, no. 61 (2007): 637–56; and Hélène Tessier, "O retorno do hereditario em psicanàlise: Dimensao axiologica das escolhas epistemologicas," trans. Luis Maia, *Percurso* 42 (June 2009): 9–18.

64 I. Grubrich-Simitis, "Zum Verhältnis von Trauma und Trieb," Psyche 41 (1987):

The phylogenetic hypothesis emphasizes an internal factor in the constitution of the sexual unconscious. However, the origin of this factor is not only biological; it is attributed to hereditary sources that originated in traumatic experiences lived by humanity in its primal stage. The fantasies of threats of castration or of seduction correspond to events experienced by our distant ancestors. Even if, as heredity, the transmission of these experiences is biological, it is not merely an inscription in the body. It requires the symbolic mediation of language to carry it from one generation to the next. The role that Freud assigned to phylogenetic disposition and to hereditary, primal fantasies, notably castration and the murder of the father, ends up as the dominant factor in his theory.[65]

Representatives of traditional orientations are often concerned that contemporary interest in external factors will cause us to lose sight of the primordial role of fantasy and of the attack of the drives in the formation of psychical life. By attributing primal contents to the unconscious, contents that would coincide with the contents of myths, particularly the myth of Oedipus, the traditional orientation can account for the content of the fantasy that acts as the psychical representative of the drive without relying on relationships with external factors. So, the notion of primal contents of the unconscious allows representatives of this orientation to remind us that in psychoanalysis, the external factor should never be considered independently of the fantasmatic treatment imposed on it by the subject. While this is true and important, it does not imply the existence of primal content for the unconscious. Nevertheless, that is the solution retained in the phylogenetic hypothesis in

992–1023; I. Grubrich-Simitis "Trauma oder Trieb—Trieb und Trauma: Wiederbetrachtet," Psyche 7, no. 61 (2007): 637–56; and Hélène Tessier, "O retorno do hereditario em psicanàlise: Dimensao axiologica das escolhas epistemologicas," trans. Luis Maia, Percurso 42 (June 2009): 9–18.

65 Grubrich-Simitis, "Trauma oder Trieb."

which myth is identified as the source of universal unconscious contents. This solution belongs to the irrationalist tradition. It also raises problems on the ethical level insofar as myth denies the historical character of domination. Nevertheless, let us specify that in psychoanalysis reference to myth is not necessarily the mark of an irrationalist tendency. Myth does have a function that metapsychology can account for. For example, Laplanche holds that myth serves as a code for translation. More precisely, myth serves to bind the anxiety arising from the drives by giving it a form and a representation. The issue is different if myth is considered either as a priori content of the unconscious or as the psychical equivalent of the sexual unconscious. To adopt either of those positions would be to endorse a theory assigning myth an originary status. But the role of theory is precisely the critical deconstruction of the description of myth as ahistorical.

Thus, although it is in a different lineage than the AngloSaxon current, which is generally closer to social constructivism and pragmatism, the traditional current has its own affiliation with the irrationalist tradition. The idea that there could be an originary, ahistorical unconscious, an unconscious whose contents would be independent of what is repressed by the individual, is an idea that can be placed squarely within romantic irrationalism: Think for example of Richard Wagner's themes and the passion for the originary that animates not only his music but also the texts of his operas. In the same way, interest in myth—including originary myths, the critique of progress, and the rupture between culture and civilization—is the source of many romantic leitmotivs seen not only in Wagner but also in philosophy, for example in Nietzsche or Spengler.[66]

---

66 György Lukács, *La destruction de la raison*, vol. 2, *L'irrationalisme modern de Dilthey à Toybee* (Paris: L'Arche, 1958).

Phylogenetic theory refers to an originary prehistory. This prehistory goes beyond the human sphere. It emerges out of a cosmic phenomenon, the glacial era, which would have provoked the murder of the father of the primal horde, whose corollary would be the affirmation of the universality of Oedipus and of the castration complex.[67] Even without this myth of origins, to consider Oedipal triangulation, tied to the traditional family, as a fundamental characteristic of humanity is to consider it a natural phenomenon, independent of social organization, power relations, and, importantly, the historic aspects of gender domination. Such a tendency has considerably impoverished the notion of sexuality, which, in the classical current, has adopted the normative aspects of sexual difference, the traditional family, the dominance of the phallus, and the privileged role of the paternal function[68] in the structuring of law and of formal thought. In this psychoanalytic current, amorous relations in an adult mode and sexuality in the popular sense of the term have, for all practical purposes, become synonymous with sexuality in psychoanalysis.

The mythical conceptions of anatomy, sexual difference,[69] and parental roles that are found in the traditional orientations have earned accusations of sexism and phallocentricism for psychoanalysis. Since they think that the concept of the sexual unconscious necessarily shares the normativity of the traditional orientations, many representatives of the Anglo-Saxon orientations, influenced by culturalist theories and feminist thought, have repudiated references to the sexual unconscious. Others have simply

---

67 Grubrich-Simitis, "Trauma oder Trieb."

68 Although the traditional current increasingly emphasizes psychic bisexuality and the absence of a real relation of the term "phallus" to the penis or of the term "paternal" to the biological sex of the parent, it is necessary to recognize that the attachment to terminology marked by phallocentrism is not fortuitous.

69 For Lacan (1966), for example, sexual difference is the true vector of the drive.

amalgamated the two currents and brought an object-relations perspective to the interpretations of the sexual unconscious based on Oedipus and sexual difference, without really resolving the contradictions their position raises at an epistemological level.

The description of differences between the two currents reveals that where the sexual unconscious is concerned Laplanche's theory can be distinguished from each. Unlike the Anglo-Saxon current, Laplanche insists on the centrality of sexuality in psychoanalysis. His theory does not emphasize the relational or intersubjective character of the infant's relations with their adult caretakers but rather emphasizes messages sent by those adults, messages that are compromised by the adults' sexual unconscious. Unlike the classical current, Laplanche's theory rejects the idea of an originary unconscious whose contents preexist the individual's history of repression. Furthermore, Laplanche's theory differs from both in setting aside the hypothesis of an originary unconscious of endogenous, biological, psychological, or hereditary origin, while adopting a specific definition of infantile sexuality that is not tied to erogenous zones, to parental sexuality, or to sexual difference.

It is now time to describe this theory in a more systematic way.

2
Sexuality and the Condition of Becoming Human: A Description of the General Theory of Seduction

In addition to in anatomy and physiology, humans differ from animals in many other ways: language, reason, morality,[70] the capacity to produce the necessities of existence[71] (Marx). Psychoanalysis emphasizes sexuality, highlighting those characteristics specific to human sexuality and the central role played by fantasy. From the psychoanalytic perspective, fantasy's central role explains why sexuality appears as invasive: It penetrates all human behaviors and is one of their determining factors. Laplanche took up this fundamental Freudian contribution and systematized its consequences. He offered an explanation for the origin of infantile sexuality that takes into account both its fantasmatic character and its indissoluble link with the other activities of the soul, including thought: "The general theory of seduction seeks to give an account of the genesis of the psychosexual apparatus of the human being, starting from interhuman relationships and not from biological origins. The human psychical apparatus is above all wedded to the drive, to the sexual drive (in the form of both the life and death drives). The somatic *instincts* are not denied, but they are neither the origin of *infantile* sexuality nor involved in the genesis of the repressed unconscious.[72]

We have underlined points at which Laplanche's epistemological

---

70 Paul Ricœur, in M. Canto-Sperber *Dictionnaire d'éthique et de philosophie morale* (Paris : Presses Universitaires de France, 2004).

71 Karl Marx in e.g. *The German Ideology* 1845-46

72 Jean Laplanche, "Three Meanings of the Term 'Unconscious,'" in *Freud and the Sexual*, 204.

orientation is linked to the rationalist tradition. These converge in a foundational element of the GTS, namely the realism of the unconscious. This postulate responds to a basic requirement of rationalist thought: that of a reality existing independently of consciousness. In the GTS, the unconscious is not made up of desires, emotions, or beliefs—in other words, it is not made up of subjective productions—of which we are unaware. On the contrary, the GTS argues that the unconscious possesses the reality of a thing, and as with other things, its contents escape the logic of meaning and of communication. But the realism of the unconscious does not imply that its source is "natural"—or material. The unconscious does not have a biological substrate, except insofar as it is rightly attributed to a human being endowed with a biological constitution, which includes sensory and motor functions and a body that reacts to excitation. The unconscious is of the order of fantasy, in both its form and its content. The postulate of the realism of the unconscious also does not imply that its contents come from a transcendental source or a source that might be considered as transcendental, such as myth or culture. On this count Laplanche is faithful to the rationalist perspective, rejecting the idea that culture or myth could exist before humans. It is not a matter of contesting the fact that, in each singular existence, society exists before the individual or that humans are essentially social beings. It is a reaffirmation of the historical character of culture and society: Man created myth, not vice versa.

1. The General Theory of Seduction and the Translational Theory of Repression

While dismissing the hypothesis of an unconscious whose universal contents draw upon the depths of atavistic myths, Laplanche's theory does not deny the existence of a situation common to all humans, a situation that sets in motion the process of humanization. This situation, which for Laplanche is the only universal and "unchangeable" situation, is that of the relation of a child with an adult who signifies without realizing what he is signifying.[73] This situation is a situation of seduction. This fundamental anthropological situation is the foundation both of Laplanche's metapsychological theory and of his theory of analytic practice.

a) The Fundamental Anthropological Situation

Even where the fundamental anthropological situation (FAS) is well known, it is often poorly understood. What is typically forgotten is that within the framework of the GTS, the FAS is described exclusively from the perspective of psychoanalysis and not from the perspective of psychology. Though the FAS is based on an anthropological fact, a fact that comes from outside of psychoanalysis—namely the fact that the little human being cannot survive without the presence of adults or older children who take care of it—and although the GTS is founded on the FAS, the FAS does not emphasize this point. It does not focus on the child's dependence, its "helplessness" with respect to the adult, but rather on the fact that, because of this dependency, the simultaneous presence of nursling and adult is inevitably an asymmetrical relationship. This asymmetry is characterized by the fact that the adult is the only one of the two protagonists who has a sexual unconscious.[74] In the ordinary context of caretaking, the adult addresses messages to the child. By definition these messages are compromised by the adult's sexual unconscious, in other words, by

---

73 Jean Laplanche, "Trauma, Translation, Transference and Other Trans(es)."

74 According to Laplanche, the dissymmetry of the FAS is the only possible justification for the dissymmetry on which the action of the analytic cure is based. It is not, at least from a legal perspective, a dissymmetry based on a relationship of dependence.

the adult's fantasies. The simultaneous presence of a child who still lacks a sexual unconscious and an adult who has one constitutes a necessary condition for the formation of the child's sexual unconscious and thus also the framework within which the process of its humanization is activated.

Before continuing the description of the formation of the unconscious in the GTS, it is useful to pause to examine three essential elements of the GTS.

1) The first concerns the distinction that must be made between the fundamental anthropological situation in the GTS on the one hand and the early relationship between parent and child to which relational, Winnicottian, and intersubjectivist theories refer. These theories also place the adult/child relationship at the source of the nursling's psychic life. As we just said, what distinguishes these theories from that of Laplanche is the definition and the role of the sexual dimension and more specifically of the seduction inherent in the enigmatic character of the sexualized messages coming from the adult. Let us recall here that sexualized does not mean sexed and that the sexualized messages in question are messages laden with the adult's polymorphous infantile sexual fantasies. In other words, perverse fantasies, more precisely sadomasochistic fantasies. In contrast, the intersubjectivist theories focus their attention on relational schemata that are acquired (or learned) by the nursling and that go on to structure its affective states. The mother/child unity described by Winnicott constitutes a relational unity in which there is an exchange of affects of which the mother is not necessarily aware—in passing let us note that, in this

theory, the emphasis is on the role of the mother, which leads either to biologizing the theory or to anchoring it in a socially overdetermined familial relation. In relational theories, the notion of the unconscious refers principally to affects or thoughts of which the subject is unaware, which are considered sexual to the extent that they relate to themes considered sexual (erogenous zones, primal scene, castration, Oedipus, feelings of love). This is a different conception of the unconscious than that which is found in the GTS. The theories of Winnicott and Laplanche are located in two different metapsychological and epistemological universes. Winnicott's theory primarily concerns the *self* and, consequently, concerns identifications within the register of hate and love.

2) The second essential point is the notion of the message. It is crucial to realize that, in the FAS, Laplanche is not concerned with events, with facts, or with actions, whether they involve the adults or the surrounding world, but only with their mediation by the messages. This is why the theory refers specifically to the messages of the adult,[75] messages—most often initially nonverbal—that make up aspects of such facts, actions, and events, as well as more direct messages.[76] The concept of "message" is central to Laplanchian metapsychology. It constitutes the key to psychical

75 This constitutes another difference from relational theories and notably from Winnicott's theory.

76 This is why humans usually interpret events, including natural events, as messages. Why me? The need to find a basis in a communication—a reason, a meaning—for an event that has none and yet has a strong effect. A message to be translated remains less worrying than a blind force with which one cannot communicate.

> reality—in other words, to an invasive reality, laden
> with infantile sexual fantasies. Let us examine the link
> between the message and psychic reality.

Psychic reality should not be confused with psychological reality. This is a confusion prevalent in psychoanalysis, and it can also be found in Freud. Laplanche writes, "On the basis of a robust 'realism,' Freud always distinguished between two types of reality: material external reality, to which we accede by perception, and psychological reality, corresponding to perceptions of what emanates from within, initially feelings of pleasure-unpleasure, then affects, and finally representations, fantasies, logical arguments."[77] [77]Nevertheless, psychological reality is not the equivalent of psychic reality. The latter, although it largely corresponds to the reality of fantasy, cannot be reduced to either its representational or its affective side. In fact, Laplanche stresses that, in contrast with psychological reality, psychic reality is unique to man. It does not constitute subjective reality. In this respect, Laplanche adopts a rationalist position for a double reason: On the one hand, he firmly supports the delimitation of psychoanalysis's epistemological field as a theory concerned with the aspects of psychic life that are specifically human. On the other hand, by refusing to reduce psychic reality to its subjective dimension, he reaffirms one of the postulates of dialectical rationalism that consists in recognizing a reality independent of consciousness—in other words, a reality irreducible to subjectivity.

Concerning the first postulate, Laplanche argues that psychological reality is not exclusive to the human soul. "Psychological reality," he writes, "is not specific to the human

---

77 Jean Laplanche, "The Forces at Play in Psychical Conflict," in Between Seduction and Inspiration: Man, 108.

being. It develops in every living creature, growing in complication with the complexity of the central nervous system."[78]

The second postulate leads back to a fundamental element of the process of sexualization in the GTS. The theory insists that the sexual unconscious can arise only from something that is already sexual. Therefore, although psychic reality is in part determined by the sexual unconscious, it cannot be formed starting from an early form of psychological reality. The sexual unconscious must have its source in the psychic reality of another human, in whom a sexual unconscious is already an active presence. But, to remain within the rationalist dialectic, this other human must not be reduced to the subjective or presubjective understanding that the child could have of him or her. If that were the child's understanding, the reality of this other human would vanish into the consciousness of the child who perceives him. This is why Laplanche emphasizes the problem raised by the Freudian description of different forms of reality. Laplanche notes that there is "something lacking" among the forms of reality described by Freud, "something which would prevent the reduction of the other to the subjectivity of the person who receives the representation of the other and would guarantee the representation's strangerness."[79] What is lacking is the category of the message. The message, writes Laplanche, constitutes "a third order of reality not alongside material reality and psychological reality but transverse in relation to them,"[80] a reality that has its own materiality. The message "is not necessarily verbal, or even integrated into a semiotic system, but it is always inscribed in a [signifying] materiality."[81] This materiality is called a signifier—

---

78 Ibid., 108n160.

79 Jean Laplanche, "The Unfinished Copernican Revolution," op. cit.

80 Laplanche, "Forces at Play in Psychical Conflict," op. cit. 110.

81 Ibid., 111.

which is to say that it "makes a sign"—even while the materiality as such escapes the sphere of meaning. Destined to polysemy, the message evokes translation. Furthermore, the message necessarily implies an address from the other and thus the intervention of the other. In this way it creates an opening not only onto alterity but also onto objectivity and thus is located at the foundation of the Copernican conception of psychoanalysis in which we find the general theory of seduction.

The third key point concerns the historical dimension that the FAS introduces in the sexual unconscious. As we have said, the asymmetry that characterizes this primal situation arises from the fact that the child, unlike the adult, is not yet endowed with a sexual unconscious. It therefore presupposes a time in which the child does not yet have an unconscious. The fact that there not yet any question of a soul, of a psyche in the psychoanalytic sense, does not mean that the child is devoid of soul in the Aristotelian sense or of psychic life in the psychological sense. Laplanche's theory delimits the epistemological field of psychoanalysis: It is complementary to the sciences that study psychic life at this stage of existence, sciences psychoanalysis recognizes as fully legitimate. This prepsychoanalytic time is essential to the delimitation of the epistemological field of psychoanalysis for which primal repression marks the entry point.

b) Seduction and Repression

The FAS brings together two conditions that enable primal repression: the asymmetry between the adult and the child and their simultaneous presence. The messages—both verbal and, above all, nonverbal—that the adults address to the child in the course of ordinary, everyday interactions are already compromised by their sexual unconscious. The compromised part of these messages is sexual, since it comes from the adult's unconscious infantile sexuality. In this respect and for this reason, these messages are enigmatic. Thus, for the adult, the compromised aspect is unconscious by definition.

For the child, the adults' messages are not received and captured by any single agency of the psychoanalytic topology. At the stage that precedes repression, it cannot yet be a question of agency or of mental process, in the psychoanalytic sense of the term. This is why Laplanche describes the reception of the message by the child as an implantation. The message, which is itself freighted with the adult's infantile sexual fantasy, implants itself in the child's "psychophysiological skin."

The psychophysiological skin refers to the psychological life of the child, or psychic life in the nonpsychoanalytic sense, and to its relations not only with sensation but also with fantasmatization, in this case with the possibility of a psychological reality but not with a psychic reality. Laplanche writes:

> What we propose is to give a full place in metapsy-
> chology to processes that are irreducible to auto-
> centrism: those whose subject is simply the other.
> Not a metaphysical other or some "little other"
> (Lacan) but the other of originary seduction, first
> of all the adult other. Central among such process-
> es is implantation. By this I wish to show that the
> signifiers brought by the adult are fixed, as onto
> a surface, in the psychophysiological "skin" of a
> subject in which an unconscious agency has not yet
> been differentiated. It is these signifiers that are re-
> ceived passively that are the object of the first active
> attempts at translation, residues of which make up
> the primally repressed source-objects.[82]

82 Jean Laplanche, "Implantation, Intromission," trans. Luke Thurston, in *The*

Implantation in the psychophysiological skin constitutes a trauma of external origin. This may give rise to fantasies, since the possibility of a psychological reality (but not a psychic reality) exists for the child at this time. For the same reason, such fantasies do not have a precise topological status. These fantasies then provoke an upheaval of internal origin. They thus become "auto-traumatic" and set repression in motion.[83]

The GTS accords a determining place to primal repression in constituting the division of the soul. Moreover, it is this division that gives psychoanalysis a unique perspective on the conflictual character of subjectivity. The division comes about in this way: The adult's message, because of the unconscious sexual fantasy that compromises it, induces a pressure to translate it. Laplanche writes, "I see the origin of the temporalization of the human being in the 'drive to translate,' and I situate the motor of this process not in the translator but in the internal, atemporal, simultaneous imbalance of the enigmatic message, which provides the force of a 'to be translated.'"[84] The first attempt at translation results in a partial failure, since the adult's message cannot be fully translated. That which remains untranslated triggers the work of primal repression. Primal repression makes possible subsequent translation of messages—and the secondary repressions that follow from them— since, in separating the untranslated from the translated, it has also constituted the translator.

The compulsion to translate that Laplanche calls a "drive to

Unfinished Copernican Revolution, op. cit..

83 Jean Laplanche, *The Unconscious and the Id*, trans. Luke Thurston and Lindsey Watson (London: Rebus, 1999), 65. [Ed note: The notion of autotraumatizing appears in the lecture of January 10, 1978, substantially before Laplanche adopted the GTS, rejecting his previous conceptualization of 'leaning-on', and so before changes in his theorizing of primal repression.]

84 Jean Laplanche, "Seduction, Persecution, Revelation," in *Between Seduction and Inspiration: Man*, 40.

translate" is another aspect of the way the GTS lies within rationalism. It keeps repression within the sphere of interhuman relations as well as within the epistemological field of psychoanalysis. The drive to translate is inherent in communication and in the category of the message as Laplanche emphasizes, writing: "The force of self-translation—that *Trieb zur Übersetzung* or drive to translate, to use Novalis's phrase—derives its power not from the translator but from the thing left untranslated or inadequately translated, that thing always demanding a (better) translation."[85] It does not come from the child, whose ego is not yet constituted. It is thus essential to describe primal repression in terms that do not imply the intervention of the ego. Laplanche writes: "We should, in fact, insist on this: primary repression is correlative with the constitution of the ego, whoever it is who says 'I.' The imperative, then, is managing to think a process that is not in the first person, nor even, perhaps, in any person at all."[86] The movement of closure from which the formation of the ego follows has not yet taken place.

Primal repression thus has a double consequence. On the one hand, it creates the sexual unconscious out of the untranslated remains of the message that, because it is outside the logic of meaning and communication, takes the form of unconscious things.[87] On the other hand, in founding the unconscious as a domain separated from the rest of the psyche, it begins to create the division of the soul, which, from then on, has two parts that are opposed: the sexual unconscious and the beginning of the ego.

Let us look more closely at the kernel of the sexual unconscious that is formed in this way. The untranslatable elements that are

85 Jean Laplanche, "Temporality and Translation," op. cit.

86 Laplanche, "Seduction, Persecution, Revelation," in *Between Seduction and Inspiration: Man*, 30.

87 Jean Laplanche, "A Brief Treatise on the Unconscious," in *Between Seduction and Inspiration: Man*, 63–64.

the compromised parts of the message become "a waste product of certain processes of memorization."[88] These waste products remain in the soul as "designified signifiers," stripped of reference or meaning, no longer representing anything but themselves.[89] As a consequence, the translational theory of repression implies a realism of the unconscious: The untranslated remainders, the "waste products" of translation, become the "thing-representations." Like things, they possess characteristics that place them outside of the relationships between humans: Impervious to time, they cannot be integrated into a logic of meaning or communication. They are in no way a subjective production. These foreign bodies, which begin as external, become internal, acting on and attacking the individual from within.

Primal repression involves two moments in time. It prefigures the double temporality of psychical processes. On the one hand, there is an exogenous time, the time when the message is sent by the other and received by the child, and on the other hand, there is an endogenous time, the time when traumatism becomes auto-traumatism and provokes repression. The moment in which the compromised message coming from the external other is transformed into an internal source of excitation corresponds to the movement of auto-translation set in motion by the enigmatic character of the message. To occur, primal repression thus requires the onset of this "auto" time. The reflexive moment (*auto/selbst*) is that of fantasy and, consequently, what prefigures autoeroticism. It is what makes the drive a sexual drive. Let us recall as well that, in terms of grammar, this time corresponds to the reflexive middle voice:[90] the voice that, according to

---

88 Ibid., 63.

89 Ibid., 64.

90 Neither active nor passive, action in the middle voice is accomplished both by

Freud, represented the model for the constitution of masochism.[91]

The advent of "auto" time is equally necessary for the constitution of the ego, since it is the formation and subsequent retrenchment of the id, following repression, that institutes the ego.[92]

What we have just described is the translational theory of repression, a theory also necessary to account for the origin of what Laplanche calls the "unconscious enclave,"[93] an enclave formed by messages that have brought about a radical failure of translation. These messages, thus, are not repressed and remain unassimilated, prepsychotic. In addition, other messages awaiting translation can be found in this unconscious "enclave" that becomes both a "zone of stagnation" and a "zone of passage or transit."[94] The formation of the unconscious enclave does not trigger the process of humanization and temporalization by primal repression or the formation of the sexual unconscious and the ego. However, pathways do exist from the unconscious enclave to the sexual unconscious.[95]

It is time now to revisit one aspect of the description of the translational hypothesis. Primal repression, as a condition for "becoming human," is, as we have said, a historical process. It thus presupposes a preliminary, prepsychoanalytic state in which the child is immediately open to the world and present to his or her surroundings. The child possesses a consciousness, but it is a consciousness that Laplanche qualifies as "nonthetic."[96] Primal repression marks the point at which the soul enters into the field

---

and upon the subject.

91 Sigmund Freud, "Repression," in *SE* 16:128.

92 Laplanche, *Unconscious and the Id,* op. cit. 65.

93 Laplanche, "Three Meanings of the Term 'Unconscious,'" op. cit. 203–222.

94 Christophe Dejours, *Le corps, d'abord* (Paris: Éditions Payot & Rivages, 2001).

95 Ibid.

96 Laplanche, *Unconscious and the Id,* 64.

studied by psychoanalysis: It constitutes the moment at which the domain of self-preservation, which includes not only physical needs but also tenderness and attachment, is taken over by the ego. From there, it is overrun by psychic reality, linked to the action of the sexual drive. This moment has a philosophical importance. It introduces infantile sexuality and its perverse components, notably sadomasochistic ones, into the conception of subjectivity.

c) Repression, the Ego, and the Process of Humanization

The unified form of the ego, the result of psychic conflict, is the form of the individual's psychic dimension generally used in the disciplines that study the phenomena of the soul and social relations. Therefore, it is important to clarify the relationship between the ego and repression.

1)   The ego must not be confused with rationality. In Freudian theory, the ego includes both the rational and the irrational parts of the soul. It has two sides: a "metaphorical side,"[97] the identificatory side that Freud describes as a "a precipitate of abandoned objectcathexes"[98]—this aspect of the ego corresponds to the irrational part of the soul, to the *self* of Anglo-Saxon psychoanalysis—and a "metonymic side"[99] in which, for Freud, the ego constitutes the agency in contact with the exterior world.[100] We have seen that, in the general theory of seduction, this function is assigned first to other entities but that the ego eventually takes charge of it, at least

---

97 Jean Laplanche, "The Derivation of Psychoanalytic Entities," in *Life and Death in Psychoanalysis* (Baltimore: Johns Hopkins University Press, 1976), 135.

98 Sigmund Freud, *The Ego and the Id*, in *SE* 19:29.

99 Laplanche, "Derivation of Psychoanalytic Entities," 134.

100 It should not be forgotten either that the ego is also mostly unconscious. Laplanche's theory accounts for unconscious aspects of the ego in a different way from Freudian theory. We will examine this point in the next section, devoted to sexuality.

in the psychic order. From this perspective, the ego tends to be "hegemonic" and to invest libidinally the reality called "exterior."[101]

2) The GTS reaffirms the essentially psychic nature of the ego. As such, the ego is defined not only by its form, energy, and mode of action but also by its contents. The ego, as translator, tends to binding of affects and representations.

The constitution of the ego, like that of the sexual unconscious, is one of the conditions of "becoming human." The role of primal repression in the formation of the ego explains the centrality of sexuality. Laplanche poses the question this way: "Why, after all, is sexuality given priority over the alimentary or the need for security, for instance?"[102] The interdependence of the formation of the ego and of the sexual unconscious partly answers this question. Repression, as the element that triggers the "process of humanization," accounts for the fact that it is through "sexuality that the human being breaks free of the biological order."[103] Sexuality, in the general theory of seduction, "opens directly onto the question of the other and, in the case of the child, onto the adult other in his or her strangerness."[104] So, "the other person is considered as primary in [the subject's constitution]—a primacy not only postulated in theory but implicated and experienced in the transference."[105]

2. Sexuality, the Ego, and the Primal Position of Masochism

Laplanche's theory revolves around two themes: translation and seduction. These terms both reveal the primacy of the other in his conception of the sexual unconscious. Translation supposes a first

---

101 Laplanche, "Forces at Play in Psychical Conflict," op. cit. 112–116.

102 Laplanche, "Unfinished Copernican Revolution," op. cit.

103 Christophe Dejours, *L'évaluation du travail à l'épreuve du réel* (Paris: INRA, 2003).

104 Laplanche, "Unfinished Copernican Revolution," op. cit.

105 Ibid.

interlocutor who speaks, writes, or signifies in a language different from the language of the recipient of the message or in a code that is unknown to this second person. Seduction implies that a person other than the one seduced is at the source of the process.

These two terms also provide information about Laplanche's epistemology. As we have said, the term "translation" leads back to the context in which the sexual unconscious is constituted and in which psychoanalytic investigations take place. In practice, this context does not depend on facts or events. It is not constituted by physiological phenomena or instinctual functions. Rather, it is the specifically human context of interhuman communication: messages, including nonverbal messages.

The reference to seduction foregrounds the sexual aspect of the process. We have already defined the sexuality that is in question. It is the polymorphous infantile sexuality that ends up invading all activities, including sexuality and sexual relations in the everyday sense of those terms. Infantile sexuality is called infantile for two reasons: For the adult, it is the sexuality whose genesis goes back to the enigmatic messages received from adults during childhood; for the child, it is the infantile sexuality of the adult that provokes the construction of the child's own sexual unconscious, which is infantile by definition. This description fails to provide a satisfying explanation for a number of points. Why is this sexuality defined, even in Freud's *Three Essays on the Theory of Sexuality*, as perverse and polymorphous? What is it that defines this sexuality as "sexual"? In other words, what is "sexual" about sexuality?

a) *The Primal Position of Masochism: What Is "Sexual" about Sexuality?*

Such questions run throuhout Laplanche's theorizing. They are raised notably in relation to the therapeutic action of clinical analysis and thus lead back to the fundamental situation that Laplanche defines as a situation of seduction: "The universal and originary situation I posit at the foundation of all human relations is that of seduction. This term, in the generalized sense I give to it, includes a considerable number of variants, with adults (from being seduced by a lover to the inherently seductive dimension of analysis itself) just as with children (in childhood or precocious seduction). But beyond these situations that are still, despite how common they are, contingent . . . what we are trying to isolate is the essence of the phenomenon of seduction."[106]

That the "seductive" is sexual seems self-evident. Whatever definition we give it, seduction presupposes a sexual component. As will be clarified later on, in the FAS, the presence of a sexual unconscious in the adult and the absence of one in the child implies, if only on the level of logic, activity by the adult's sexual unconscious. But this fact provides no indication about the nature of the sexual. What makes the sexual unconscious sexual? How does a fantasy become sexual? What is sexual about it? Is it its content? Its mode of action? If the adult's sexuality corresponds to the enigma of the message, what is sexual in the enigma? Why and in what sense is an enigma sexual?

To answer these questions, it is useful both to take another look at Freud's theorizing of sexuality and to revisit the question of how the sexual drive is constituted in Laplanche's GTS.

In *Three Essays on the Theory of Sexuality,* Freud defines infantile sexuality as polymorphous and perverse. It's important to emphasize that masochism occupies an important place in his theory of sexuality. Unlike psychiatric theories of the end of the nineteenth

---

106 Jean Laplanche, "Sublimation and/or Inspiration," in *Between Seduction and Inspiration : Man.*

century,[107] in which masochism was considered degenerate or even constitutional sexual pathology, Freud asserts that it is a component of all human sexuality. In fact, he asserts that, in the form of an opposition between activity and passivity, masochism and sadism occupy a central place in the sexual organization of every individual.[108] On this basis, psychoanalysis reveals not only the general role of masochism in sexuality but also the importance of fantasy in every sexual activity, as well as the determining role of representation in sexual excitation and sexual satisfaction. The role of fantasy is particularly prominent in masochism. In "'A Child is Being Beaten': A Contribution to the Study of the Origin of Sexual Perversions," Freud showed the importance of the fantasy of chastisement in the masochist mise-en-scène.[109] Theodor Reik also thought the masochist cannot do without imagination, that daydreaming constitutes the essence of masochism.

Laplanche radicalized the Freudian conception of masochism. The GTS places masochism at the origin of human sexuality. This is explained as follows: According to Laplanche, the turning back on the self, autoeroticism, is what distinguishes the drive as sexual. The drive becomes sexual at the moment it becomes autoerotic. As we have already said, autoeroticism and, more precisely, "turning round upon the subject's own self"[110] is characteristic of masochism.

107 Notably the theorizing of Richard von Krafft Ebbing. See Hélène Tessier, in M. Marzano, *Dictionnaire de la violence* (Paris: Presses Universitaires de France, 2010).

108 Jean Laplanche and Jean-Bertrand Pontalis, *The Language of Psychoanalysis* (New York: Norton 1973 [1967]). [In 1905 Freud wrote: "The most common and the most significant of all the perversions—the desire to inflict pain upon the sexual object, and its reverse—received from Krafft-Ebing the names of 'sadism' and 'masochism' for its active and passive forms respectively." *SE* 7:157.]

109 Sigmund Freud, *SE* 17:175–204.

110 Freud, "Repression," 147. ["Psycho-analytic observation of the transference neuroses, moreover, leads us to conclude that repression is not a defensive mechanism which is present from the very beginning, and that it cannot arise until a sharp cleavage has occurred between conscious and unconscious mental

But the GTS considers the turning back on the self from a different perspective than that of Freudian theory. Laplanche does not describe the turning back, which he calls "auto-time," as a mode of autoaggression tied to an activity that initially is muscular activity exerted by the child on its surroundings. Rather, it is described as a reversal of the fantasy. In "La position originaire du masochisme," Laplanche writes:

> Elsewhere, at the site of what we have termed reflexive masochism or the middle voice, we have located a fantasy that has a properly masochistic content in the "passive" sense: my father is beating me. As we have already stressed, the point is that the process of reversal cannot be conceived of solely at the level of the content of the fantasy, but must be seen *in the very movement of fantasmization*. Moving to the reflexive is not only or not even necessarily to give a reflexive content to the fantasy's "expression," it is also and above all to make the process reflexive, to make it internalize or enter into oneself as fantasy. To fantasize aggression is to turn it on oneself, to self-aggress, at the moment of auto-eroticism that confirms the indissoluble link between fantasy as such, sexuality and the unconscious.[111]

Thus, the originary position of masochism remains consistent with the requirement for "Copernicanism" that Laplanche sets as a condition for the validity of metapsychological hypotheses. Since the child's sexual drive has its source in the invasion of

---

activity—that the essence of repression lies simply in turning something away, and keeping it at a distance, from the conscious. This view of repression would be made more complete by assuming that, before the mental organization reaches this stage, the task of fending off instinctual impulses is dealt with by the other vicissitudes which instincts may undergo—e.g., reversal into the opposite or turning round upon the subject's own self."]

111 Jean Laplanche, "The Originary Position of Masochism in the Field of the Sexual Drive" in *The Unfinished Copernican Revolution* op. cit. 91

sexual fantasy, the turning back on the self is not strictly speaking a real turning back; it is more of passage from the exterior to the interior, from a message that excites coming from the exterior to an internal source of excitation that, henceforth, acts from within. This passage is accomplished by fantasmatization. The turning back "is conceived of solely at the level of the content of the fantasy but must be seen in the very movement of fantasmatization."[112]

The originary position of masochism in the GTS is another aspect of its adherence to the rationalist tradition. In making fantasmatization the point at which the intersubjective dimension becomes an intra-subjective[113] dimension in which excitation finds its source, Laplanche gives an explanation of masochism that remains within the specific field of psychoanalysis. In the beginning, masochism is both fantasy and the movement of fantasmatization.[114]

b) *The Unconscious and Masochism: Fantasy and the Sexual Drive of Death*

The adult's sexuality that the child confronts in the FAS was itself also implanted in a traumatic way. In the adult too, masochism sealed sexuality; that is, the fantasmatization and the turning on oneself were the first moment of sexualization for the adult too. Therefore, the compromised enigmatic part of the adult's message is also the product of infantile polymorphous perverse sexuality, and consequently for it too, sadomasochistic aspects play a determining role. The "auto" time that Laplanche posits as a

---

112 Jean Laplanche, "The Originary Position of Masochism in the Field of the Sexual Drive" in *The Unfinished Copernican Revolution* op. cit. 91

113 These terms must be used with caution because, strictly speaking, one could not speak of human subjectivity, in the philosophical sense, before the original repression. It is rather a psychological subjectivity, in the sense of the psychological reality, which is not limited to humans.

114 Cf. Jean Laplanche, "Masochism and the General Theory of Seduction," in *The Unfinished Copernican Revolution* op. cit.

condition of possibility for the sexual drive is an autotraumatizing time. "Fantasy," writes Laplanche, "is traumatic because it is internal: It is a source of excitation and incitement."[115] It constitutes "the first psychical pain."[116]

The autoexcitation resulting from fantasy unfolds in the temporal sequence of repression: activity/passivity. Repression requires two steps: The first, implantation, is characterized by passivity. As we have said, the passivity does not arise from the child's dependence on the adult. Although carried along by this dependency, the passivity comes from the nursling's inability to "master what is coming to it from the adult world."[117] The time of passivity is followed by a time of activity, the time when fantasy becomes an internal source of excitation, in other words, a time of autoerotism. This sequence of passivity and activity, in particular the obligatory character of the passive time, evokes the masochist fantasy, in the everyday sense of the term: The idea of submitting to something of which one is not the cause makes up a central element of masochist ideas and of masochist autoerotic activity.

It is necessary, however, to recall how Laplanche understands passivity. That is another important way his theory is connected to rationalism. To clarify the way in which the conception of passivity in the GTS differs from the usual conceptions, which define it as a function of observable behavior, Laplanche, citing Baruch Spinoza, refers specifically to the Cartesian tradition. On this point, Laplanche distances himself from the empiricist perspective. "Passivity and activity," he writes, "are not defined by whoever

---

115 Jean Laplanche, "Reparation and Penal Retribution: a Psychoanalytic Perspective," in *The Unfinished Copernican Revolution* op. cit.

116 Laplanche, "The Originary Position of Masochism in the Field of the Sexual Drive" in *The Unfinished Copernican Revolution* op. cit.

117 Jean Laplanche, "Trauma, Translation, Transference and Other Trans(es)," in *The Unfinished Copernican Revolution* op. cit.

initiates an act, or by penetration, or, indeed, by any behavioral element. Passivity is completely composed of the inadequate ability to symbolize what happens to us due to the action of the other."[118] With this definition, Laplanche also disrupts the equivalence too frequently established in psychoanalysis between passivity and femininity, which constitutes a major weakness in many psychoanalytic conceptions of masochism. What is repressed in originary repression is passivity in Spinoza's sense of "inadequate ideas" to the extent that, according to Laplanche, these ideas evoke the untranslatable part of the message of the other.

As we have said, primal repression accounts for the creation of the sexual unconscious. This process reproduces itself: Secondary repressions happen; the primal repressed exerts a force of attraction on the process and content of translation of the sexual unconscious both in its more bound and in its more accessible form. Considered from the perspective of the soul as a totality, the mode of action of the sexual unconscious is itself masochist, since it functions in the mode of attack and since the ego, which has taken charge of vital interests and self-preservation, is its object.

The mode of attack is free or unbound energy always in search of excitation. Laplanche's "sexual drive of death" represents the most unbound form of action of unconscious fantasy that results from the residues of the translation of the enigmatic messages. It involves "a fixed and unchangeable fantasy, not historicized but designified, senseless and inaccessible by any direct means—a fantasy that is truly primal, that can only be seen through its conscious perverse derivative effects," which are principally masochistic.[119] So the

---

118 Ibid., 263.

119 Jean Laplanche, "Interpretation between Determinism and Hermeneutics: A Restatement of the Problem," trans. Luke Thurston in *The Unfinished Copernican Revolution*; "The So-Called Death Drive: A Sexual Drive," in *Between Seduction and Inspiration: Man*, 174; and "Sublimation and/or Inspiration," trans. Luke Thurston

death in question in the death drive is not the death of the other but the death of the ego, which can ultimately lead to the death of the individual. From this perspective, psychoanalysis accounts for the "demonic" aspects of the human soul, the aspects that escape binding and mastery, the *Lucifer amor* that defines the soul just as fundamentally as does reason. It is interesting to compare the conception of the origin of the sexual drive according to which the enigmatic signifier, "the source-object of the drive, is 'stuck' in the envelope of the ego like a splinter in the skin"[120] with other conceptions that highlight the central role of masochism in the human soul while also linking masochism and the demonic. The metaphor of the splinter is not only a metaphor for a sting of desire in the ordinary sense. For example, in Saint Paul, "the splinter in the flesh" represents "the angel of Satan" that leads to the taste for suffering—for "weakness, outrages, calamities, persecutions."[121] Nevertheless, masochism and the demonic are not only negative and destructive. They are both constitutive of the soul, and both are concerned with resistance and human emancipation. We must consider their dynamic function in the development of subjectivity.[122]

c) Masochism, Repression, and the Ego

The idea of "Satan," of an "adversary," who attacks the ego, should not lead us to presume that, in contrast to the sexual unconscious, the ego is not sexual. As we have said, libidinal energy exists as much in the ego as in the Id. In the ego, however, this energy functions according to a principle that tends toward totalization and

in *The Unfinished Copernican Revolution*.

120 Jean Laplanche, "Masochism and the General Theory of Seduction," trans. Luke Thurston, op. cit.

121 2 Cor. 12:7–10.

122 See Tessier, in Marzano, *Dictionnaire de la violence*.

narcissistic binding. Nevertheless, the ego is also tied to masochism, which comes from two sources: its causal origin in repression and its construction by way of identifications. The ties between the ego and repression are particularly important in explaining how psychoanalysis contributes to the understanding of subjectivity, and subjectivity is the fulcrum of every action in the social field.

As we have often repeated, the "auto" time necessary for setting in motion the first attempt at translation, for the repression that follows, and for the constitution of the sexual unconscious is also necessary for the constitution of the ego since it is the formation and, following repression, the subsequent retrenchment of the id that divides the soul and thereby also creates the ego. "Auto" time is equally essential to the ego for another reason. The ego is an agency that temporalizes itself. Yet, temporalization requires a consciousness that can reflect on itself: The consciousness of one's own consciousness is in effect what makes possible the constitution of one's history.[123] Thus, mediated by repression, "auto" time acts on the side of the ego. It leads from consciousness to self-consciousness—in other words, to an "auto-consciousness," to a consciousness that is conscious of itself, that is concerned with itself, and that in this way is simultaneously subject and object.

Given the causal relationships between reflection, autoeroticism, and masochism, one can conclude that masochism's originary position in the formation of the sexual drive also implies an originary position for masochism in the advent of the ego. Such a connection between desire, masochism, and self-consciousness is found in the famous slave/master dialectic that Hegel (1807) presents as a process of the objectification of self-consciousness. It is significant that, in order to account for the division and the doubling of consciousness, Hegel requires a reflection that, taken

---

123 Jean Hyppolite, Études sur Marx et Hegel (Paris: Marcel Rivière, 1955).

out of its philosophical context, resembles the well-known themes of masochistic fantasies, even masochistic mise-en-scènes. Indeed, masochistic scenes of the BDSM genre are defined by the master/slave scenario in terms that are startlingly similar to those Hegel uses.[124]

The ego displays other ties to masochism. It represents the interests of self-preservation and of narcissistic binding. It is constructed from identifications in a way that uses the codes of translation available to it, codes that are full of the sadomasochistic fantasies that run through the culture. Therefore, it reflects the heteronomous social goals that, given masochism's central role in the process of humanization, are most often in the service of conformism, complacence, and even submission with respect to the most influential tendencies.

d) The Essence of the Sexual

To return to the question "What is sexual in sexuality?" we must revisit the conception of sexuality in the GTS. The self-attacking sexuality— what Laplanche calls the *"sexual"* —is not the only form of sexuality. Sexuality covers a wider area. In addition to the sexual unconscious, an unbinding force, it also includes narcissistic sexuality, which is a binding force. In its unbound form, sexuality corresponds to the sexual death drive, to *Lucifer amor* as described by Freud. This "sexual" attacks the ego from within, works according to the rule of unbinding, separates affects from their representations, seeks the shortest path to excitation. It makes its presence felt in the form of anxiety. Narcissistic Eros, the binding and totalizing sexuality, is also erotic, but it arrives later, after the ego is already formed. It belongs to the identificatory functions of the ego, from "its irrational side," and refers to the "self" of the

---

124 Tessier, in Marzano, *Dictionnaire de la violence*.

Anglo-Saxon schools.[125] Narcissistic sexuality encompasses many aims. Laplanche emphasizes that, for purposes of binding, its identificatory aspects provide it only with codes that come from the outside:

> We can categorize the synthetic action of the ego into two rather different types. According to a first mode, which might be called Gestaltist, the ego imposes unity on what is diverse and anarchic in the drive by way of the ego's unitary and specular form. This type of binding is eminently narcissistic and, as such, rather crude. The ego unifies what is diverse either directly or through simple term-to-term opposition. We rediscover here the character traits (stubbornness, orderliness, thriftiness) Freud invokes and privileges in the case of anal eroticism. . . . Here what I want to emphasize is that character formations activate a simple (and even simplistic) type of binding, one that is narcissistic and only minimally inserted into networks of meanings.
>
> The other mode of binding, however, is accomplished by way of symbolic connections. I have proposed the idea that the binding of the enigmatic message coming from the other is accomplished on the model of a translation, thanks to elaborate or elementary codes furnished to the child by his surroundings. That translation is not only a matter of first messages and primal acts of repression. Throughout childhood (and, we should add,

---

125 Jean Laplanche, *The Temptation of Biology: Freud's Theories of Sexuality*, trans. Donald Nicholson-Smith (New York: Unconscious in Translation, 2015 [1993]), 80.

throughout a psychoanalysis), there are episodes of detranslation and retranslation, governed by après-coup. In contrast with the stupidity of the narcissistic-Gestaltist type of binding, in which a unifying totality is imposed without mediation, there is the complexity of symbolizing links and symbolic systems in which—if one needs philosophical point of reference—object and concept are necessarily correlated with scenarios, propositions, and judgments.[126]

Nevertheless, while the narcissistic Eros does make up part of sexuality, Laplanche reminds us that, in all the forms of binding that belong to narcissistic sexuality—in other words, those that in varying degrees result from the workings of the sexual life drives—"what again and again come to be bound are the multiple components of the sexual death drive, sadism and masochism."[127] This affirmation implies the primacy of the sexual, which is to say the primacy of polymorphous, perverse infantile sexuality over narcissistic sexuality. It implies that the sexual—or erotic—character of narcissistic sexuality comes from its ties to the sexual unconscious. For Laplanche, there is only one libidinal energy: the libidinal energy at the origin of the drive. What distinguishes the sexual life drives from the sexual death drives is their mode of operation: free energy and "the circulation of nonmeaning" for the sexual, bound energy and "circulation of meaning" for narcissistic Eros. Without the prior constitution of a sexual unconscious, there would not be narcissistic sexuality since there would be nothing to bind. So, the response to the question "What is sexual in sexuality?" must be sought in the sexual unconscious and in the correspondence

126 Laplanche, 'Sublimation and/or Inspiration,' op. cit. 264–65.
127 Ibid., 263–64.

between the sexual death drive and sadomasochism.

Therefore, what is sexual in human sexuality is masochism. In its autoerotic dimension, masochism is indissociable from fantasy and representation, the two foundational features of human sexuality. It also corresponds to the nature of fantasy, whose essence, as Laplanche reminds us, is not to be translated but to be fulfilled (*zu erfüllen*).[128] And yet the masochistic fantasy has a direct path to excitation since it works on the individual and since it is, in itself, its own fulfillment. Masochism would also be at the source of "the essence of the seductive," of seduction in its anthropological dimension, being defined as a relation of activity and passivity.[129]

The originary position of masochism in sexuality defines the terrain on which psychoanalysis and the social field come together. It allows the identification of what, on the anthropological level, gives power and domination such potential for seduction. At the social level, the issue of masochism becomes a moral question since masochism, insofar as it is a fundamental dimension of human sexuality, constitutes the psychical mediation that promotes conformism, submission to authority—including despotic and illegitimate authority—and collaboration with violence. One could ask if the scandal of the sexual, often evoked in psychoanalysis, does not, contrary to widespread opinion, consist in the scandalous primacy of sadomasochism in the regulation of social relations. In this case, the drive renunciation that Freud described would imply first and above all a renunciation of the satisfaction that masochistic fantasy provides.

---

128 Jean Laplanche, "Goals of the Psychoanalytic Process," in *Between Seduction and Inspiration: Man*, 195.

129 Laplanche, "Temporality and Translation," op. cit.

3
Rationalism and Psychoanalysis

We have emphasized several ways in which Laplanche's theory is connected to the rationalist tradition. Now we must define rationalism and provide the reasons that connection with this philosophical tradition serves as a criterion for justifying the choice of one theory over another in the human sciences, notably in psychoanalysis.

1. Rationalism and Democracy

The idea of connecting rationalism and the justification of epistemological choices arises in large part from the conviction that it has become essential to challenge both the relativism that reigns in this domain and the discredit in which the notion of truth is held in current cultural conditions. At least on a moral level, every intellectual enterprise, a fortiori scientific work, must be shaped by a demand for truth. In research in the social sciences, the dominant positions have turned away from this demand: The function of truth, embodied in knowledge of reality, has given way to the goal of strategic mastery of the environment, including the social environment. The systematic linking of research to social needs (again, it would be necessary to discuss how and by whom these needs are determined) has become an epistemological linkage. The objective of research increasingly emphasizes an operational focus on the goal and the impact of interventions.[130] This type of attitude is associated with neopragmatism, which considers truth to be immanent in experience: The truth of a proposition is made

---

130 M. Freitag, *Le oubli de la société: Pour une théorie critique de la postmodernité* (Quebec: Presses de l'université Laval, 2002), 98–99.

concrete by its utility and its capacity to produce desired effects.[131] A systematic examination of the relationship between postmodern cultural conditions and modes of validation is not necessary to be able to identify the synergy between neopragmatism and speculative logic, a synergy whose effect is to establish a form of validation based on practical success and/or on public recognition.[132] Such validation is based on auto-referentiality: The value attributed to an activity is proportional to the value one believes will be attributed to it by the people whose judgement counts. This position is dangerous: It subjects validation of a position to social relations that favor the positions held by the those who are most influential.[133] The search for truth presupposes the exercise of critical thinking and so is always a potential threat to dominant interests.

Besides, the truth of a theory, or what is considered the truth of a theory, is based not only on criteria intrinsic to the theory's domain. Epistemological choices do not find their sole justification in epistemology, which is tightly linked to philosophical conceptions. In 1936, in an essay written in honor of Freud's eightieth birthday, Thomas Mann wrote: "Scientific objectivity[134] is or should be a *moral* fact. . . . One might strain the point and say that science has never made a discovery without being authorized and encouraged thereto by philosophy." The validity of a theory should be the object of an argument that goes beyond both its discipline and a strictly epistemological examination.

---

131 [Ed note: As Laplanche says, "[This is to] do injury to a great tradition, the tradition of pragmatism as an epistemological stance. It would require forgetting, that while true pragmatism does take success as a criterion, the success in question is the success of thought and not the success of obtaining of an immediate material effect." Jean Laplanche, *New Foundations for Psychoanalysis* (New York: Unconscious in Translation, 2016), 12.]

132 A. Orlean, *Le pouvoir de la finance* (Paris: Odile Jacob, 2009), 209.

133 Christophe Dejours (1998–2006).

134 *"Die Voraussetzungslosigkeit der Wissenschaft ist ein moralisches Faktum oder sollte es sein."* ["Scientific freedom from assumptions is or should be a moral fact."]

For Laplanche, the question of truth is present from the beginning in scientific research, in the human sciences as well as in psychoanalysis. "The affirmation of truth or falsehood," he writes, "cannot be limp or imprecise."[135] According to him, a modern psychoanalytic theory must present itself within a problematic; it must situate interpretative and critical choices in relation to Freudian theory. The choices to which such an approach leads are also "commanded" by a historical reading and by the "fundamental demands" that the psychoanalytic discovery imposes on theory.[136136] Laplanche's position is not a pragmatic position. Both by the method that he proposes (critical and historical analysis) and by its mode of validation (subordination to a demand that exceeds its disciplinary sphere), Laplanche places himself within a rationalist perspective. In the following chapter, we will see how "Copernicanism," which constitutes the "fundamental demand" in whose terms he measures the validity of theorization in psychoanalysis, belongs to the dialectical tradition of rationalism. But for the moment let us return to rationalism and its status as the criterion of evaluation for Laplanche's theory.

a) Rationalism, Reasoning, and Rationality.

The definition of rationalism offered here is not a philosophical but a political conception. It has been developed in relation to psychoanalytic theory, relying on the questions that Laplanche's thought poses for psychoanalysis and also in an attempt to understand the disappointing evolution of psychoanalytic conceptions of the soul and of social phenomena. Though developed in relation to psychoanalysis, this definition may come to be used in

---

135Jean Laplanche, *Between Seduction and Inspiration: Man* op. cit. [Translation modified.]

136 Jean Laplanche, "The Death Drive in the Theory of Sexual Drives" in *The Unfinished Copernican Revolution*, op. cit. 351-366

other fields, but that is not the objective of this book. This is why the principal aspects of rationalism examined here will be described in connection either with psychoanalytic concepts or with certain trends in Freudian and post-Freudian psychoanalytic theory. In relating this definition to psychoanalysis, I will take account of sources that have served as foundations for the definition of rationalism developed here.

This definition is inspired by the writings of Thomas Mann, writings that bear witness to the author's political trajectory and the transformation of his philosophical positions in light of his experiences of Nazism and his reflections on its rise. The definition also relies on the essays of Victor Klemperer, who sought to demonstrate the incompatibility of Nazism and rationalism. These two authors described how irrationalism, as well as the cultural attack on reason and the intellect that accompanied Nazism, constituted the necessary condition for Nazism's success.

Today we are again witnessing a contempt for reason and the intellect that is disquietingly evocative of the situation described by Thomas Mann in 1929. In observing "the strange psychological coexistence of unbelief and hatred of belief" that surrounded him, he wrote, "[We see] a pervading and dominating anti-idealistic and anti-intellectual tendency to do away with the primacy of mind and reason, to despise mind and reason as the most fruitless of illusions, and to elevate in triumph, as the original authorities over life, the powers of night and darkness, the instinctive (*das Instinktive*) and the irrational."[137] The forces of darkness, the instinctive and the irrational, may express themselves differently than they did at the beginning of the twentieth century, but they are no less present. In

---

137 Thomas Mann, "Freud dans l'histoire de la pensée moderne," trans. Louise Servicen, in *Sur le mariage, Lessing, Freud et la pensée moderne* (Paris: Aubier-Flammarion, 1978. Originally published as "Die Stellung Freuds in der modernen Geistesgeschichte."

the liberal societies of our era, the aestheticization of violence takes different forms than it did before, but we are witnessing the same persistent debasement of thought, the same discrediting of critical reflection, the same anti-intellectual propaganda that contributed so much to "the rising tide of the insignificant" described by Castoriadis.

This text of Mann's from 1929 had been written for *Freud's birthday and entitled Freud's Position in the History of Modern Culture*.[138] For Mann psychoanalysis explores "the demonic nature [and] dark regions of the soul" but believes that this exploration does not arise out of a "negation of spirit and a nature-conserving sycophancy in regard to instinct [but rather] stand in the service of a revolutionary victory for reason and spirit, for a future and for enlightenment." On the contrary, the exploration appears, , to be guided by an element of spiritual order that saves it from being deformed by an "intention hostile to the mind." In Mann's view, Freud gave "sexuality a character of revolutionary spirituality" in which one can find the search for a "new order of life, deserved and rendered secure by consciousness and resting on emancipation and truth."[139] Nevertheless, Mann was concerned by the ease with which psychoanalysis could fit into an apolitical anti-rationalism, the heir to a romantic atmosphere whose consequences for culture and social life Mann challenged. It seemed to Mann that psychoanalysis contained what was necessary for "those movements that tend to place knowledge under feeling and thus serve the retrogressive powers . . . without asking permission of the new science, to enter into a bold and deceitful bond with it." This concern proved to be well-founded: Even if psychoanalysis was not tied to the rise of fascism, such as it appeared in Europe in the first half of the

---

138 Ibid.

139 Ibid. [Translation modified.]

twentieth century, one can still acknowledge that Thomas Mann's fears were largely realized.

In fact, psychoanalysis has at times affirmed the existence of primal, originary fantasies and myths whose universal contents would then constitute the bedrock of the sexual unconscious. It has adhered to the phylogenetic hypotheses, and several of its current schools continue to refer to them today. The irrationalist tendencies in psychoanalysis are now reincarnated in new forms, forms that appear less dogmatic and more democratic; that glorify the emotions, presumed to bear unmediated authenticity; and that have a blind confidence in the affects, described as the leading, major, and unclarifiable factor in the process of change, as well as those forms that return to biological conceptions of the soul and the mind.

These new forms of irrationalism are associated with subjectivist convictions that mistrust the idea of truth. As such, they belong to a lineage from which the great complexes of psychoanalysis emerged, and similarly they contribute to distracting psychoanalysis from its interest in the unconscious. Moreover, despite its willingness to describe itself as subversive, psychoanalysis has shown that it can work just as well with conservatism and even the reactionary, notably in family matters. Its normative attachment to the traditional family, to the sexual distribution of parenting roles, and to gender stereotypes, its mistrust of egalitarian claims, its abstract, apolitical, and archaic reference to law and the "Law," have for a long time treated every attempt at critical analysis with lofty contempt.[140] More recently, the reintegration of psychoanalysis into the ranks of relational psychology and theories of attachment, as well psychoanalysis's courtship of neurosciences and naturalist conceptions of mind and consciousness, is leading it into the

---

140 Tessier (2007).

currently dominant orientations of philosophies of the mind.

The question of the rationalist affiliation and the political significance of Laplanche's theory arises in this context. Of course, we must be careful not to conflate rationalism with logical thought, understanding, and rationality. Reason is irreducible to intellectualism, and rationalism does not imply that human thought and action is solely determined by reason. Human thought and action are not cut off from emotions.[141] The opposition that some see between the dryness of understanding and the plenitude of life, sensibility, and affect is eminently reductionist. Rationalism does not consist in ignoring the different components of the human soul, or considering the soul as separate from the body. Rather, it demands an account of these components based on reason, more precisely, on discursive reason. Rationalism starts from the principle that everything human is intelligible, even if this intelligibility is far from immediately apparent. In a way, the debate about faith in scholastic theology, in which an Aristotelian rationalism played an important role, provides a point of comparison that can clarify the terms in which the problem presents itself. On one side of that debate, there were those who were certain that faith, as an ineffable experience, flows from an adherence to a first truth, a belief founded on passion. On the other side, there were those for whom faith, as a virtue, belongs to the category of the good (*vis appetitiva*) and not to an intellectual approach based on the category of truth.[142] The latter position accepts the difference between faith and reason. From that perspective, it is through the perfection of feeling that man draws closer to God, but it is through science and knowledge that

---

141 The theory of Antonio Damasio (1995) on this question implies a restrictive view of rationalism as we define it in this book. According to this definition, one cannot claim to be rational in the absence of emotions and feelings.

142 I. Schüssler, *La question de la verité* (Lausanne: Payot, 1982).

man's reason approaches perfection.[143] The goal of this example is not to connect rationalism and theology but rather to show that, historically, the rationalist tradition has also been at work in disciplines that involve phenomena that lie outside of reason. It has done so by distinguishing between faith and knowledge while showing that one cannot go directly from affective adherence to an intellectual search for truth.

From this point of view, we can see how the enduring attachment of psychoanalysts to the idea of an primal unconscious, ahistorical in its origin, whose symbolism, which is called universal—and incidentally is tightly linked to the patriarchal family and the primacy of the phallus—constitutes the key to its inscription in humanity, is better characterized as an act of faith, in the sense of an affective belief in a truth considered as a given, than as an example of critical reasoning. From this perspective, it belongs to the irrationalist tradition, as it even includes the terms of the medieval debate over the nature of faith.

The notion of an innate, primal unconscious is part of the traditional current. The traditional current, because it focuses above all on drives, consisting of primal contents defined in relation to phylogenetic theories, often appears as a bulwark preserving psychoanalysis from the relational drift that, for its part, eliminates reference to a sexual unconscious acting as a force alien to the subject. From this perspective the association of the traditional current with irrationalism was not seen as a problem. On the contrary, it was considered an asset. Opposition to rationalism became a decisive argument in psychoanalytic debates, the rationalists being seen as rejecting Freudian pessimism, fragmentation of subjectivity, and alterity of the unconscious. Therefore, the relational current could be condemned a rationalist tendency.

---

143 S. Tugwell, *Albert and Thomas: Selected Writings* (New York: Paules Press, 1988).

The definition of rationalism proposed in this book does not support this type of dichotomy. In fact, the relational theory has its own association with irrationalism, one that is just as significant as that of the traditional metapsychology. Notably, it covers up an undeniable dimension of human conduct, indeed, a dimension whose elucidation is a goal of psychoanalysis. This dimension is the part of human behavior that resists education, that, despite all efforts, often works against the best interest of the person herself, and that shows itself capable of an astonishing cruelty. By avoiding this dimension, the relational current shirks a fundamental requirement of rationalism: the requirement to confront aspects of reality that exist independently of our subjective consciousness. As Thomas Mann insists, the humanism that is the foundation of rationalism requires that rationalism must "include all the science of the depths and the demonic in its veneration of human mystery."[144]

It is important not to conflate rationalism with logical thinking. Pragmatism, for example, is associated with irrationalism through its functionalist traits, through its theory of knowledge, and through the naturalization of epistemology that it implies. Nevertheless, it is a logical theory whose mode of exposition has nothing irrational about it. In the same way, Lacanian structuralism in psychoanalysis is affiliated with irrationalism even while being an altogether logical system. The irrationalist affiliation of Lacanian theory comes, importantly, from an uncritical acceptance of the difference between the sexes as the vector of the drive and as the structural foundation of the unconscious. Similarly, despite its logical form, Lacan's mathematical modeling of phenomena of the soul belongs to the irrationalist tradition. This affiliation stems from the fact that

---

144 Mann, "La philosophie de Nietzsche à la lumière de notre experience" ["Nietzsche's Philosophy in the Light of Contemporary Events"], in *Les Maîtres*, trans. Louise Servicen and Jeanne Naujac (Paris: Grasset, 1976).

a purely formal system cannot account concretely for the soul's contents or their unpredictable character.

For their part, neurological explanations of phenomena such as love, violence, empathy, or morality do not necessarily present themselves in an esoteric form. Nevertheless, despite reference to the natural sciences, they belong to a scientistic ideology more than to a form of scientific reasoning concerned with accounting for phenomena in their totality. The line between science and scientistic ideology is easily crossed. Science then becomes a vision of the world that imposes itself in an uncritical way, impervious to critique: "Despite the dimension of incompleteness and indefinite progress that characterize it, the scientific ideal was quick to make a leap toward the absolute, and a dream of a total mastery."[145]

Like mathematical models, cognitivist theorizing runs into the problem of content, especially when it tries to give an account of thinking, especially when looking for the links between the material, biological, or physical aspects of thought processes and the semantic or representational aspects. It tries to resolve this problem by integrating the interpretive function of thinking linked to intentionality into its formal logic. This integration is accomplished by emphasizing the physical changes that arise from the emotional states that provoke interpretative activity. Cognitivist theorizing thus remains within the limits of a theory of knowledge based on representation.[146] Yet, representation leads back to the subject-object problematic, precisely what psychoanalysis has taken as its mission to call into question. In psychoanalysis, the subject is neither unified nor given. Laplanche writes:

---

145 Jean Laplanche, "Psychoanalysis in the Scientific Community," in *Between Seduction and Inspiration: Man*, 153.

146 F. Varela, *Initiation aux sciences cognitives*, trans. P. Lavoie (Paris: Seuil, 1983).

> The term "representation" necessarily refers to a
> subjectobject problematic, which is—perhaps—that
> of a "theory of knowledge." The latter is situated in
> a perspective I have called Ptolemaic. Psychoanal-
> ysis must assume as its starting point the fact of
> interpersonal communication as well as the priority
> within it of the sexual message emanating from the
> other. The messages "I love you" and even "Eat to
> make me happy" convey neither information about
> the world nor a problem concerning the congru-
> ence of a "representation" and what is "represent-
> ed." . . . The problem, in the unconscious, is not the
> intentional relation between a representation and
> its object (the representation of a thing) but the fact
> that a part of the message becomes "designified"—
> that is, a kind of "thing" (and a cause).[147]

The definition of rationalism that we uphold here must respond
to a double requirement: that of critical thinking and that of fidelity
to the specific aims of psychoanalysis in its questioning of notions
of subject and of subjectivity as well as the objections it raises to
reflexive philosophy and to the theory of knowledge. This definition
must also be based on what psychoanalysis adds to the perspectives
of other human sciences in order to contribute to a more complete
and thus more concrete description of reality.

b) Rationalism: Principal Traits

Rationalism implies a relationship to reality, to a reality that exists
independently of our consciousness and is not reducible to it.[148]

---

147 Jean Laplanche, "Psychoanalysis: Myths and Theory," in Between Seduction
and Inspiration: Man, 301.

148 Such a definition raises the question of idealism as a form of rationalism,
especially the idealism of Hegel. For the discussion of this question, I refer to the

Nevertheless, it is necessary to avoid understanding rationalism abstractly, making it a "suprahistorical principle" inherent in human thought.[149] Rationalism itself has a history. The philosophical thinking that in one era concerned fundamental claims later, because of new ways of considering reality in its political context, served as a basis for irrationalist developments. A historical understanding of rationalism has consequences for the way one conceives of the demarcation between rationalism and irrationalism. History implies change. To be desirable, change must, in one way or another, involve improvement, progress. This is why placing the distinction between rationalism and irrationalism in its historical context allows the inclusion of the idea of emancipation. As György Lukács wrote, reason consists principally in "not avoiding the necessity of the present: Reason and unreason are together like the recognition of progress and its repudiation."[150] For example, in its time, the materialism of the Enlightenment thinkers was a revolutionary and emancipatory materialism. It was a materialism opposed to feudal categories in which privileges were justified because they were attributed to a transcendental source. Holding the same positions two centuries later, in a social context in which domination no longer has the same religious or economic basis, has nothing progressive about it and ends up supporting positions completely in line with the established order. This historical conception of rationalism belongs to a dialectical tradition characterized by the concept of totality. Totality represents the requirement to grasp the determinations of a reality along with their necessary—that

---

work of G. Lukács, *The Destruction of Reason* (1958–59), which consistently refers to the historical character of rationalism and to the political role of theory as a function of the economic, sociohistorical, political, and cultural context of thought.

149 György Lukács, *Histoire et conscience de classe*, trans. K. Axelos and J. Bois (Paris: Minuit, 1960), 148.

150 Lukács, *La destruction de la raison*, 2 vols. (Paris: L'Arche, 1958–59).

is, noncontingent—interrelations. So to answer the question of whether a position is rationalist, it is necessary to examine what the position excludes from critical thinking, as the exercise of reason is necessarily confined within each partial system the position addresses. Therefore, totality always stands out as the principal challenge for rationalism, considered as a requirement of thought. Until the modern era, theology marked the limit of rationalism. Consequently, thought could envision only a partial reality. "The ultimate problems of existence"[151] were considered beyond the reach of human understanding. Modern rationalism has increasingly questioned this limit and so has been able take up the claim of liberty in the social field while challenging the political authority granted to feudal economic and legal structures whose legitimacy was attributed to a transcendental source. The rationalist thought of the Enlightenment involved a secular or, rather, secularizing foundation that brought into the field of science and into political debate sectors previously largely restricted to the religious sphere. From then on, the theory of law demanded the sovereign not place himself above the law but rather submit himself to it.

Rationalism thus requires that the links between different spheres of thought, activity, and reality not be hidden or obscured. This is also a necessary condition for transformation. We have seen that theory can act on reality only if thinking considers reality in its totality, understanding it as concrete reality. Yet it is as true today as it was in the past that there is a tendency to examine reality through the lens of partial systems and a reluctance to open up their borders. For example, the idea that laws of the market are inescapable and not the products of or subject to human will. Similarly, there is the growing reliance on management theories to assess performance or "returns" based on criteria independent of the content and purpose

---

151 Lukács, *Histoire et conscience de classe*, 145.

of the work being performed.[152] In these two cases, by considering reality from a partial or fragmented perspective excludes part of the reality from critical analysis. If one accepts the possibility of a self-contained object of study and considers this object as separate from and independent of other objects and other fields, the foundations of the discipline that studies the object in question escape scrutiny. The questions that might shake up the discipline are not recognized as pertinent or even seen. Only rules internal to the system are available for critical examination. Thus, the work of understanding is confined to rules internal to the discipline and not the rationality of the discipline and the logic of the system it serves in the frame of global reality. To stand at the frontiers of a system of study and open it to concrete reality is to repatriate into the realm of reason that which was hidden, living within the sphere of the irrational.

This description may seem abstract, but its subject is concrete situations, as we can demonstrate with a few examples. In human affairs, irrationalism consists in accepting the idea of a primal origin whose own origin goes unexamined or whose original foundation cannot be discussed. In law, for example, jurists often cannot avoid conceiving of juridical norms as givens and working with them within a closed system.[153] Furthermore, there are many examples in literature of the irrationality of logic applied to a system whose rationality cannot be questioned. Thomas Mann's *Magic Mountain* is a prime example. This work describes a closed world, cut off from work and action, whose internal rationality hangs on a perilous social irrationalism. One might also cite the work Nikolay V. Gogol,

---

152 Christophe Dejours, *L'évaluation du travail à l'épreuve du réel* (Paris: INRA, 2003) and Chirstophe Dejours, *Travail vivant*, vol. 2, *Travail et émancipation* (Paris: Payot, 2009).

153 For example, in the theory of *Grundnorm*. Moreover, lawyers are not inclined to establish links between private law or criminal law and the recognition and protection of property rights, although these links are fundamental when, for example, it comes to examining the legitimacy of the tax rules of a market economy.

in particular his short story "The Nose," in which everything unfolds with the greatest normality within a completely irrational situation: the independent existence of a nose that, separated from its owner, carries on with its own life. It goes around in a carriage dressing as an officer, conversing with people who do not confront the nose with the impossibility of its incarnation and who, most of the time, don't even seem surprised. Despite its fantastical theme, this short story presents an extremely realistic critique. It powerfully evokes the irrational foundations of an autocratic society, where fear and self-interest are the ultimate motives for behavior.

The tendency to abandon the rationalist requirements of critical thought and the openness to totality and so to close oneself within a partial reality evokes what, in psychoanalysis, Laplanche described as "endless Ptolemaic relapses,"[154] both in Freud and in the post-Freudians, which lead psychoanalysis to move away from its own project, to close itself up within a "primal" subject that the reality of the sexual unconscious should keep open to alterity. Laplanche observed that in psychoanalysis this tendency of theory to close back in on itself constituted "a parallel instance of the inevitable narcissistic closure of the apparatus of the soul."[155]

In the following chapter, we will see how to interpret this double tendency, of humans and of theory, in relation to what the GTS reveals about the structure of consciousness. In the rest of this chapter, we will examine the two limits confronting rationalist thought when it comes to taking the concrete aspects of reality into account—that is, in a complete form. These two limits appear as first "the inability to grasp totality starting with concepts formed in partially rational systems" and second "the irrationality of specific conceptual content." According to Lukács these two limits are

---

154 Jean Laplanche, "The Unfinished Copernican Revolution," op cit..
155 Ibid.

"two aspects of the same problem," which is that of dodging the moment essential to transformation.[156] How are they incarnated in contemporary psychoanalytic thought?

2. The Irrationalist Sources of Contemporary Psychoanalysis

In the preceding chapter, we described the two major currents of psychoanalysis today by grouping them under the headings of AngloSaxon, or relational, psychoanalysis and classical psychoanalysis. We said they each entail a form of the closure of the subject on itself tied to the genetic approach in psychoanalysis. They correspond to the two sources of rationalist thought described by Lukács, who retrospectively examined the tendencies of irrationalism as manifestations of what Thomas Mann called a "cultural climate" that encouraged the rise of fascism. We obviously do not mean to assert that contemporary psychoanalysis has any relationship whatsoever with fascism—whatever meaning one gives to "fascism." But it is true that philosophical and psychoanalytic theories do not arise from nowhere, but rather they are the product of the political and economic relations of their time. Furthermore, they help pave the way for the ideological forms that emerge from these relations. On the subject of Nazism, Lukács's commentary on the ties between philosophical theories, the cultural climate, and political orientations should lead us to reflect on the responsibility of anyone undertaking a work of theoretical elaboration, including the work of psychoanalytic theorizing. He wrote: "For [Nazism's] conception of the world, which has such fragile foundations, so lacking in coherence, so profoundly nonscientific and so marked by such a crude dilettantism, to become the dominant conception of the world, a certain philosophical atmosphere was required: a shattering of confidence in understanding and reason; the destruction of the

---

156 Lukács, *Histoire et conscience de classe.*

belief in progress; credulity in the face of irrationalism, myth, and mysticism."[157] One might hope that, in a climate in which "the shattering of confidence in understanding" is once again familiar to us, psychoanalysis would not support the tendency.

As is the case for other disciplines, ideologies have shaped and continue to shape the evolution of psychoanalysis. We have seen how both classical psychoanalysis and the Anglo-Saxon currents maintain ties to irrationalism. Here, of course, there is no question of addressing the ties of individual representatives of these currents to irrationalism, nor of denying the rigor of their thought. Rather it is a matter of considering the way irrationalist tendencies are introduced into psychoanalysis and of emphasizing how they correspond to general cultural tendencies. Above all, it is a matter of seeing how the possibility of submitting psychoanalysis to rationalist critique, as Laplanche did, allows us to resist a form of thought that today has become hegemonic. This critique also aims to better situate psychoanalysis within the scientific community as a discipline whose domain is necessary, but not sufficient, for the concrete comprehension of the human soul and of human behavior.

a) Phylogenesis and the Role of Origin

Phylogenesis and the idea of an innate, primal unconscious are part of cultural currents that became dominant in Germany at the beginning of the twentieth century, as is well documented by Thomas Mann's *Doctor Faustus*, completed in 1947. Shortly thereafter, Lukács demonstrated the ideological ties of those cultural currents to the economic and political context of the time.[158] The passion for the archaic, the fascination for the originary (the

---

157 György Lukács, *La destruction de la raison*, vol. 2, *L'irrationalisme modern de Dilthey à Toybee* (Paris: L'Arche, 1958).

158 Lukács, *La destruction de la raison*.

primal, the *Ur-*), which found an aesthetic form in Wagner's operas, constituted a distinctive trait of that era's culture.[159] Moreover, Thomas Mann emphasized the degree to which Wagner's quest for "the original, poetic element of the human soul, the first and simple thing par excellence, could not be satisfied with an origin weighed down, however slightly, by a debt to history." This quest for the primal was soon recycled in the political sphere, taking the place of what could have been an opening to social problems. "In the face of the problems of the hour," Mann wrote, "[where] the need for a more just economic system [is seen] as the most urgent moral duty . . . such an attitude leads to attempted solutions that in reality are loopholes and appear manifestly as mythical systems, taking the place of real social action. . . . If we translate the political jargon into psychological terms, the current formula is: 'I do not want to know anything about the social question; what I want is the folk tale [*Märchen*],' except that in politics the tale would better be called a lie."[160]

The attraction of psychoanalysis to theories of origin, like those adopted by traditional psychoanalytic anthropology, belongs to this tendency. The attraction is what stimulated Thomas Mann's fears when he evoked the possibility of a deleterious alliance between "psychoanalysis and the forces of regression and restoration." This anthropology relies on the anatomical difference between the sexes, taken as "bedrock" and as the basis of the organization of the psyche.[161] This conception implies that there is necessarily a point

---

159 The intention here is not to make a hasty generalization about the cultural context for the birth of psychoanalysis. After all, Austria is not Germany, and there were other currents in both countries, notably those related to Marxism and to the workers' struggle. The aim here is to examine the factors Laplanche sees as having led psychoanalysis to turn away, partially, from its initial project.

160 Thomas Mann, "Richard Wagner and the Ring of the Nibelung," in *Noblesse de l'esprit*, trans. F. Delmas (Paris: Albin Michel, 1960).

161 Sigmund Freud, *Analyse avec fin et l'analyse sans fin : Résultats idées, problèmes II*

at which culture rejoins nature and there finds its source. Such a position played a significant role in certain romantic currents.[162] It is eminently dangerous in the political field. To argue that biological sex and sexual difference, even in the form of a psychical bisexuality, represent "the very heart of being, its quintessence"[163] is to take a position that is quite problematic from the standpoint of reason, or mind. Furthermore, recourse to the myth of Oedipus, to the myth of the primal father of the primal horde, to castration, "consists in establishing a hierarchy in which the mytho-symbolic would be situated at a deeper, more archaic, more primordial level than what is individually repressed."[164] This solution defines the relation between the individual and society in a dubious way because it leads "to the phylogenetic hypothesis, in the strict sense of a biological inheritance, the only way to 'stuff,' if the word be permitted, atavistic experience into the center of the individual."[165]

Laplanche insisted on the importance of not confusing the formations of the unconscious with the myths used by humans in their auto-theorization, in other words, with the mytho-symbolic— whose origin is cultural—used as a translation code. He underlined the necessity of maintaining a distinction between metapsychology on the one hand and the myths and mytho-symbolic theories on the other. The latter provide schemata for translations used "to cope with the anxiety . . . provoked by the enigmatic elements coming from the adult other." So according to Laplanche, the true

---

(Paris: Presses Universitaires de France, 1988), 268.

162 A. Béguin, *L'âme romantique et le rêve* (Paris: José Corti, 1991). This theory is much older than romanticism. The idea that blood is responsible for traits of character is a theory used to justify aristocracy: the theory of blue blood (in practice, it was pale skin revealing blue veins that became synonymous with nobility).

163 Victor Klemperer, *Je veux témoigner jusqu'au bout*, Journal 1942-1945, vol. 2, 5.

164 Laplanche, "Psychoanalysis: Myths and Theory," 235.

165 Ibid.

basis of "the meta position" of metapsychology is "the extent to which it gives itself the means to account for the function of mythic constructions in the constitution of the human being."[166]

In Freud's work, the distinction between the two levels of theories gradually faded, its absence covered by the introduction of primal fantasies, by the predominance and universality of Oedipus, and by the growing predominance of castration. However, it is not correct to attribute to Freudian theory a purely irrationalist affiliation, or to attribute essentially conservative political positions to early twentieth-century psychoanalysis. When Thomas Mann mentioned "the revolutionary spirituality" that psychoanalysis attributed to sexuality, he was not thinking of the theory of primal fantasies. Indeed, on the question of dream interpretation, the approach of psychoanalysis has even been called overly rationalist, "closer to eighteenth century than to romanticism."[167] If it seems important to emphasize the growth of the place accorded to phylogenesis in Freud's work, it is because phylogenesis has been taken up in a more dogmatic way by post-Freudians and has become almost canonical in psychoanalysis, to the point that even within relational currents, for different but equally problematic reasons, modern variations of it have become dominant.

The recourse to using myth as the primal content of the unconscious puts the problem of accounting for the content of thought in an irrationalist form. To attribute mythic contents to the unconscious from the start is to empty out the question of the source of its content: The source is provided by myth. But this completely removes the myths themselves from critical analysis, and likewise their historical origin, and the question of "how myth is transmitted

---

166 Ibid., 243.

167 Béguin, *L'âme romantique et le rêve*, xxi.

or 'passed' to the child."[168] It simultaneously puts outside of consideration the issue of the function of the content of mythical thought in human thinking. For instance, by tightly holding on to a biological "bedrock" and to sexual difference, psychoanalysis tends to blind us to phallocentrism. Laplanche writes that it is imperative to work ourselves clear of the two obstacles bequeathed to us by mythology and mythologists, namely focusing on already elaborated versions of mythical narratives without dealing with how the myth is transmitted or "passed" to the child and also focusing on ethnographic myths (even if they be those of Greece) without raising the question of formations and scenarios that, *in our own time* and *in the West*, embody the mytho-symbolic function. Psychoanalysis has perhaps blinded us on this last point by attempting to impose as the sole and unique contemporary myth simplified versions, issuing from Freudian (and later Lacanian) phallocentrism.[169]

It is therefore obvious that the idea of a primal unconscious, or of primal fantasies, not only permits evasion of the problem of the source of unconscious contents as that question is considered in the tradition of rationalism but also eliminates the possibility of escaping the limits of a partial system of thought, since there is no attempt to address the origin of myth as a human creation. Myth is given a transcendental foundation that, from then on, constitutes the starting point for logical constructions and serves as the explanatory framework for the very phenomena of which it is supposed to be the cause. In other words, it constitutes an unavoidable and universal given, which cannot be subjected to critical questions. Thus, myth is placed outside any system of thought in the same

---

168 Laplanche, "Psychoanalysis: Myths and Theory" in *Between Seduction and Inspiration: Man.*, 240.

169 Ibid.

way that, in feudal law, the sovereign is above the law. This issue leads us back to the metaphor of the Copernican revolution. What were theological grounds for condemnation of heliocentrism? The fact that it didn't allow God to be placed above the world. To summarize: If the Earth is no longer the center of the universe, the universe has no center. In fact, there are multiple centers, because the mathematical equations that prove that the Earth moves around the sun also imply the vastness of the universe, even its infinity.[170] "The Copernican revolution," writes Laplanche, "to some extent, opened up the possibility of the absence of a center."[171] If the universe has no center, it cannot have a circumference. It is precisely here that the theological problem arises: In the absence of a center and thus of a circumference, God is included in the universe.[172] In other words, if the universe is infinite, there is not a transcendent world; "the beyond is part of the here-below."[173] The idea of myth as the primal content of the unconscious or accepting the existence of primal fantasies resembles a theological position for which the requirement to think of reality in its totality does not exist. Myth is always excluded from it since it is placed above the world of human reality. Myth is inaccessible to reason. It preexists historical humanity and in fact provides the condition for its possibility.

b) Irrationalism and Object-Relations Currents

One might think that the relational currents are closer to the tradition of rationalism. In fact, they are just as far removed as the

---

170 From this point of view, the Copernican revolution constitutes an unfinished revolution, since Copernican cosmology preserved a center. B. Mély, *Giordano Bruno, un visionnaire du XVIe siècle* (Mouans-Sartoux: PEMF, 1999).

171 Laplanche, "Unfinished Copernican Revolution," op. cit..

172 Cf. ibid., xxnxx.

173 Thomas Mann, *La montagne magique*, trans. Maurice Betz (Paris: Arthème Fayard, 1931), 455.

traditional current but in a different direction. Rationalism assumes recognition of a reality that exists independently of our awareness, but this is precisely what is challenged by the relational current, for which subjectivity occupies a central position. The subjectivity of the relational current is characterized by its capacity to define the real.

As we have said, the relational current includes many schools and tendencies that differ from one another but can be grouped together on the basis of their conception of subjectivity and the role they attribute to it.[174] Within this diverse current, there are four strong tendencies: the importance of the subject-object relation, the place of affect as the vector of a direct access to the real, the determining role of intuition in the apprehension of reality, and the affirmation of the irreducibly subjective nature of knowledge. From this point of view, the relational theories de facto understand psychoanalysis as a theory of knowledge. As such, psychoanalytic treatment aims to change the subject's way of understanding the object by promoting modification of the individual's subjective representations through an adequate and well-meaning object relation and, as a result, modifying the subject's self-perception and interpersonal relations, as well as representations that subject has of others and of events. This is why theories of narration and narrative creativity are important in these analytic schools: The reality that we talk about is the only significant reality. It is a reality that does not include elements that are not objects known by the subject.

Laplanche has shown that the "Copernican" project of psychoanalysis aimed precisely at escaping the philosophy

174 Some are close to transcendentalism, others close to pragmatism and to empiricism. For instance, the Winnicottian orientation, with its conception of the true self, is more clearly related to irrationalism than the tendencies that arise from pragmatism. See Hélène Tessier, *La psychanalyse americaine* (Paris: Presses Universitaires de France, 2005).

of the subject, at distancing itself from a process whereby the constitution of the human subject would be understood to take place necessarily in the first person.[175] The closure of the subject on itself implies a withdrawal into a partial system. Whatever origin or biophysiological foundation might be ascribed to such subjectivity, two aspects are excluded from critical questioning, even by psychoanalytic theory: first, how subjectivity arises out of an intersubjective relation that by definition requires two subjects who are already "subjective" and, second, how to reconcile the idea of a fragmented subjectivity with the idea of a subjectivity that brings together all the psychic agencies. How can an irreducible subjectivity grasp its own division or conflictual aspects or the phenomena of resistance that are necessary for the very idea of change in psychoanalysis?

The relational current also runs up against the question of the origin of unconscious content, but because of the way it conceives of the unconscious, this problem is generally ignored. Essentially it considers the unconscious in a descriptive way; it is not differentiated from subjectivity. It is understood as comprising affects, early relational patterns, and thoughts that are not part of subjective experience and of which the subject is not aware. When unconscious contents gain access to the realm of feelings and so to a form of reflexivity, they are produced by subjectivity or cocreated in the frame of intersubjective relations.

---

175 [Laplanche systematically explicates the idea that psychic processes such as repression, projection, etc., cannot and should not be understand in first person. He sees the need to contest solipsism and reaffirm the intervention of the other.] See particularly Laplanche, *The Unfinished Copernican Revolution*; Jean Laplanche, *The Temptation of Biology: Freud's Theories of Sexuality*, trans. Donald Nicholson-Smith (New York: Unconscious in Translation, 2015); Jean Laplanche, *Between Seduction and Inspiration: Man*, trans. Jeffrey Mehlman (New York: Unconscious in Translation, 2015).

In this way the relational schools adopt the position that we can know only what we ourselves have created. This affirmation belongs to an irrationalist tendency that acquired a considerable importance in the wake of Kant's reinterpretation of the Copernican revolution, a reinterpretation that, as Laplanche wrote, corresponds to a radical recentering of psychological subjectivity.[176] The idea that all the contents of thought are produced by subjectivity constitutes a form of irrationalism. It represents an attempt to overcome the difficulty, which appeared insurmountable, of accounting for the contents of thought in a nondogmatic way. To this end, philosophical thinking adopted the model of mathematics, in which, as Lukács wrote, the irrationality of the content provokes the reworking of the system of forms by which the content is grasped, to the effect that what initially appeared as a given comes to appear as a product of thought. Such a method is not problematic in mathematics, where "the production and possibility of understanding entirely coincide."[177] In psychoanalysis, as in other disciplines that deal with the contents of thought, postulating the subjective production of contents constitutes a solution that displaces the problem to an anterior stage without resolving it.

How does subjectivity produce content? Is it through internalization of the object relation? Through the projection of what is found within the subject? If the latter, how does what is found within the subject arise? Are those contents produced by a biological process? If so, how should we understand psychical content whose origin is biological? Should we leave in shadow the passage from sense-experience to fantasy and, moreover, to fantasy that has content? In the absence of answers to these questions, we find ourselves in the *"projectio per hiatum irrationalem"* described by

---

176 Laplanche, "Unfinished Copernican Revolution," op. cit.

177 Lukács, *Histoire et conscience de classe*, 152.

Lukács: It consists in the projections of an object "of whose birth we have no idea and, consequently, where there is an obscurity and a gap between the projection and the projected."[178]

Facts and contents always appear foreign. The idea that thinking can know only what it has itself produced, in addition to being eminently problematic at the political level, in practice inevitably confronts experience that refutes it—or that should refute it. Like traditional psychoanalysis, the relational current keeps what serves as its foundation protected from critical examination. Although it makes use of different categories than those of classical psychoanalysis, it works in the same way: accepting the specialized character of the psychoanalytic perspective while ignoring the philosophical grounding of its point of departure. Thus, it also "leaves the material substrate that is its ultimate condition of possibility in an 'unthreatened irrationality' (as 'uncreated,' as 'given') in a closed world . . . with categories of understanding that raise no problems . . . and which, in any event, are no longer brought to bear on the material substrate."[179]

In effect, both the traditional and the relational currents place psychoanalysis in a world beyond understanding. This is not the same thing as recognizing the limits of the field of psychoanalysis. It is of course well understood that psychoanalysis cannot explain all phenomena and that other disciplines must take over at the borders of the psychoanalytic field. The problem of irrationality arises when what serves as the foundation of a discipline is considered as a given that does not have to be accounted for by discursive reason. This is a "Ptolemaic" position, in the cosmological sense of the term. Psychoanalysis operates within a horizon delimited by what escapes understanding.

---

178 Ibid., 153.

179 Ibid., 153–154.

At this horizon, classical psychoanalysis finds culture – understood as an originary entity. This culture is not derived from anything. It constitutes a foundational fact.[180] The opposition culture/ civilization that was important for the Romantics[181] was taken up again, if not by Freud, then at least by a large part of post-Freudian traditional psychoanalysis—particularly the French—to the profit of a notion of culture that corresponds to the philosophical need to define it as a foundational entity, beyond the transformative action of the historical process, the notion of progress being depreciated and tied to the concept of civilization.[182]

In using the culture/civilization polarity as the axis of comparison of theories, Laplanche placed himself on the side of the notion of civilization. We can see this, for example, when he refers to Voltaire and when he comments on the different ways of translating Freud's aphorism *"Wo es war, soll ich werden."*[183] In "Responsibility and Response," Laplanche takes the side of the rationalist tradition, for which civilization is a matter of work and progress, more precisely work directed at society:

> *Wo Es war, soll Ich werden* is a formula that can be translated, depending on the context, with a sense of *Schwärmerei*, a slightly delusional enthusiasm, or of *Nüchternheit*. In the sense of *Schwärmerei*, one can say: "A subject is to come to be"; but with a cold-ness or more Freudian *Nüchternheit*: "Where id was, must ego be." That last translation (you will see

---

180 Ibid.

181 Lukács, La destruction de la raison.

182 The works of Thomas Mann between *Reflections of an Unpolitical Man* (1918) and *Dr. Faustus* (1947), passing through *The Magic Mountain* (1924), constitute a reflection on this question.

183 Here he is criticizing the Lacanian translation, *"un sujet doit advenir,"* as manifesting an unfortunate packaging.

that I often return to these questions of words, but
they are quite important; if one yields on words,
Freud used to say, one ends up yielding on things
themselves) I owe to Conrad Stein, who quite rightly invited us to note that a noun like "*Es*" or "*Ich*,"
without article, might be quite simply a partitive,
and he quoted a sentence as an example: "Where
there was wheat, we will put barley." "Where there
had been sea (as Freud phrases it), there should be
land, namely the reclamation of the Zuydersee."[184]
Which takes us in the direction of a slightly prosaic and flattened out translation: "There where
there was (some) id, (some) ego should be." And,
to continue, one might amuse oneself by pushing
the polders as far as Candide's garden: there where
there was raging sea, if you please, a bit of firm
land on which eventually to plant some tulips . . .
[ellipsis in original][185]

The relational current might not object to this "flattening"
translation, since its representatives usually take a prosaic attitude
on the matter of subjectivity. In any case, the question of the id and
the ego is not of much concern to them, since in this current, the id
is folded into the descriptive unconscious and is already integrated
into the self. To overcome the problem of the given, the problem
of facts that arise independently of subjective consciousness, the
relational current takes the path of interiority by affirming that

---

184 In referring to the Zuydersee, Freud evokes Goethe's *Faust*. Goethe is
representative of the rationalist tradition in German thought. He was also an
internationalist and a supporter of the term and of the concept "civilization":
A swamp lies there below the hill Infecting everything I've done: My last and
greatest act of will Succeeds when that foul pool is gone.

185 Laplanche, "Responsibility and Response" in *Between Seduction and Inspiration:
Man*, trans. Jeffrey Mehlman, op. cit. 143

the only reality with an effective existence is the reality created by the subject. To return to the cosmological metaphor, the relational current sees itself in a Ptolemaic world. The horizon of this world is the subject himself; the content of subjectivity is a primal fact. Perhaps it would be better to say that there is no longer a world, since the subject fills it entirely, but rather a multitude of worlds constituted by a multitude of subjects. Subjectivity creates the content of the world and, in psychoanalysis, creates the content of fantasy. The re-centering that takes place in traditional psychoanalysis lends itself more easily to illustration by medieval cosmology than does the re-centering of the relational current. The latter is more reminiscent of the post-Kantian reversal from which arise the contemporary conceptions of the freedom to contract and freedom as autonomy. Two tendencies can thus be identified in the Ptolemaic closure, two tendencies that correspond to two distinct philosophical traditions: an authoritarian and dogmatic tendency on the one hand and a pragmatic and liberal tendency on the other.

The relational current often conceives of the birth of subjectivity as a corporeal phenomenon. Motor activity, sensitivity, excitability, and neurophysiological maturation would be at the source of lived experience. Although the activity of thinking cannot be dissociated from the body, this observation does not address and still less resolves the problem of the specific content of thought. The leap into the irrational that the auto-production of contents of thought implies appears as follows: Either the content of thought is a fact, which should be taken as such, in its facticity, without our being able to account for its origin, or the content is produced by the subject following a meaningful phenomenon, and in that case, it is this phenomenon whose facticity must be accepted without it being possible to specify the relationship between the phenomenon and the specific content of thought.[186] Therefore, to give an account of how meaning is produced, it becomes necessary to call on one or another form of mysticism.

As Laplanche writes, "The locus of affect is primarily the body and secondarily the ego. Affect is the experience of the way in which the body and the ego are *affected*."[187] The rationalist requirement involves trying to make sense of the content, on the one hand, of what affects the body and, on the other, of what is susceptible to being experienced as an experience without being seen as a fact before which understanding must bow, as a fact that is immune to discursive reason and so must be accepted as a given. The category of the message allows us to avoid this pitfall.

3. Rationalism and the Category of the Message

Laplanche emphasizes the fact that in psychoanalysis the mind/body split is not a pertinent distinction; the psychoanalytic domain begins at the border between sexuality and self-preservation.[188] Both selfpreservation and sexuality are anchored in the body, but in humans both unfold in the context of interhuman communication. It is this context that makes the message the decisive category in the GTS. The category of the message also allows us to get beyond the subject/object opposition and, in so doing, to use reason to give an account of the content of fantasy.

Why refer to the unity of subject and object with regard to the contents of thinking or, to remain in the psychoanalytic field,

186 Lukács paraphrases the underlying reasoning: "Are empirical facts (whether purely 'sensory' or having their sensory character as the deepest material substratum of their actual essence), to be taken as 'given' in their facticity, or does this character of given dissolve in rational form? . . . Doesn't it lead to their being thought of as produced by 'our' understanding?" *Histoire et conscience de classe*.

187 Jean Laplanche, "A Brief Treatise on the Unconscious," in *Between Seduction and Inspiration: Man*, 85.

188 Jean Laplanche, "Drive and Instinct," in *Freud and the Sexual*, 11.

with regard to the contents of fantasy? Because the question of the rationality of contents, taken as a given, is directly related to this unity. The unity of the opposition of subject and object represents another way of expressing the difficulty of understanding the way contents are produced. An important issue in philosophy concerns the link between the subject—the thinking or knowing subject—and the content of what he thinks or knows. The object of thought seems to be an object exterior to the one who thinks it, exterior in the same way as are other humans and the objects of sensation. The problem takes on two forms in psychoanalysis: The first is that of the relation between the subject and the unconscious. Does the unconscious constitute a subjective dimension produced by the subject himself, including in the framework of intersubjective exchanges, or does it constitute a reality independent of the subject—an "objective" reality? The second form of the problem involves the contents of fantasy and can be expressed in the same way: Are these contents subjective productions, whose origin is somewhere in the body, whether in affect or in the internalization of affective relations? Or, to the contrary, do these contents have a reality independent of the subject? If the latter is the case, is this content necessarily primal, universal, and mythical? We have seen that neither of these solutions are retained in the general theory of seduction.

Subjective idealism and objective idealism attempt to overcome the subject/object duality,[189] either by relying on the subjectivity of knowledge and heading for interiority or by postulating a form of contact that would be "mind to mind, intellectual intuition," which would allow one to grasp what is an essentially transcendental object, distinct from the subject.[190] Laplanche's solution involves

---

189 This is excluding the natural sciences, in which the duality is treated differently.
190 György Lukács *The Destruction of Reason.*

neither of these alternatives. It is related to Marxist thought, which modified the position taken in objective idealism by introducing the category of practice. "The unity of subject and object," wrote Lukács, "is activity."[191] This affirmation implies that in order to account for the content of fantasy (understood as an object) in a rational way, it is necessary to start with an act and not with a fact. Furthermore, one cannot separate the question of form from that of content. Thought, or, in the case of psychoanalysis, fantasy, is not a pure form. It is inconceivable without content. Let us examine how form and content are related in Laplanche's GTS.

The fundamental anthropological situation does not constitute a fact. It is characterized by a synchronic asymmetry in which an activity is produced: the emission of a message in the frame of an interhuman communication. This activity constitutes an act, since the subject of the communication—the one who communicates—himself creates his object, the message. In addition—and Laplanche insists on this point—"the fundamental hermeneutical position is not a hermeneutic of situation or facticity but a hermeneutic of the message."[192] In the message, the world of the subject and that of the object come together. Communication "is not situated in the world of being and finitude. [It opens up a] suprasensible dimension."[193]

This "suprasensible" dimension refers to the content of the message. The translational hypothesis of repression accounts for the link between the content of the message and the content of fantasy. What the human being has "to make sense of," writes Laplanche, "is not a situation; it is sequences that are presented as already having meaning—what I call, in a general way, messages

191 Lukács, *Histoire et conscience de classe*, 157.

192 Jean Laplanche, "Goals of the Psychoanalytic Process," in *Between Seduction and Inspiration: Man*, 192.

193 Lukács, *Histoire et conscience de classe*, 157.

from adults."[194] In fact, translation does not entail only subjective production. It is created starting with a text, a message, a sign, even a nonverbal one, that is necessarily external to the subject and includes a part that brings out the "suprasensible." Furthermore, in the GTS, not only the translation but also the contents of the sexual unconscious are treated in an altogether individual way by the work of repression. Implantation "does not mean that the unconscious is simply the other implanted in me. For in between the primary intervention of the other and the creation of the other thing in me, there occurs a process called repression—an extremely complex process comprising at least two stages in mutual interaction and leading to a veritable dislocation/reconfiguration of elements (explicit and implicit-enigmatic) lived experience. Metabolization and the 'translational' point of view are the soul of the theory of repression."[195]

4. Rationalism, Political Thought, and Epistemological Choices

The two forms of irrationalism embodied in the two main orientations of contemporary psychoanalysis correspond to the forms of irrationalism that were described by Lukács as "the destruction of reason" in relation to the cultural climate that facilitated the success of fascism. These were the hard variant, the mytho-symbolic variant, and the soft variant, the liberal variant of the pragmatic tendency. In psychoanalysis, mytho-symbolic thinking places "biological bedrock" and sexual difference at the foundation of the humanization of the soul. The result is that human characteristics of the mind are not primary. They are secondary to sexuation. Such a position is difficult to accept at both the ethical

---

194 Laplanche, "Psychoanalysis: Myths and Theory," 241.

195 Laplanche, "Unfinished Copernican Revolution," in *The Unfinished Copernican Revolution* op. cit.

and the political level.[196] An anatomical or physiological difference or a mythical version of this difference is a risky basis for a theory of the soul.[197]

The soft variant of irrationalism found in the relational currents poses its own dangers. The importance accorded to the "sentimental and instinctive aspect," the insistence on "lived experience" that one finds in these currents as the basis for a theory of the soul, can also play a role in what Klemperer calls the "dethroning of reason."[198] It could seem contradictory to raise suspicions regarding the thinking behind currents that have always favored the use of the term "mind" to designate the field of psychical life and that are in many people's eyes very close to the neurocognitive sciences. Their epistemological position regarding psychological processes simplifies the critical activity relating to the contents of thought by submitting them to only the test of the emotional reactions that accompany them. It supposes an axiological leveling, as if what is felt could, on its own, indicate what is good. And yet emotion is neither more immediate nor more authentic than thought. As Laplanche has pointed out, morality cannot be derived from life.[199] When lived experience and feelings play the determining role in the evaluation of a situation, the attention given to truth is diverted to subjective convictions,[200] which inevitably support conceptions of the world belonging to each person's individual sensibility, conceptions for which the criteria of evaluation remain outside critical scrutiny.

---

196 Victor Klemperer, *L.T.I.: La langue du IIIe Reich*, trans. E. Guillot (Paris: Albin Michel, 1996).

197 Replacing sex with race or ethnicity makes the risk is even more evident. The reasoning, however, is the same.

198 The market, for example, acts in an irrational way, and investors are encouraged to be guided by their perceptions, which are themselves dependent on how their actions are supposedly perceived. Orlean, *Le pouvoir de la finance*.

199 Cf. Laplanche, *Temptation of Biology*, 129.

200 Schüssler, *La question de la verité*.

Such conceptions correspond to the concept of *Weltanschauung*. As Lukács writes, to consider lived experience as a superior mode of understanding reality or as the foundation of hermeneutics "necessarily leads to a vision of the world (*Weltanschauung*)" in the pejorative sense of the term.[201] In the ethical and political spheres, the relativism of *Weltanschauungen*, visions of the world, as a major tool for the analysis of the justness of decisions and actions constitutes an ambiguous basis on the intellectual level—and even more so on the moral level.

Though we need to avoid getting caught up in a demagogic reference, here it is useful to consider Klemperer's commentaries on the importance of the concept of *Weltanschauung* in the discourse of the Third Reich.[202] Klemperer wrote that this concept translated the aversion of Nazi ideologues for the notion of system into the idea of a universal truth. It represents, according to him, "the truest opposition to the philosopher's act, because philosophy is an activity of reason, of logical thought, the worst enemies of Nazism," which wanted "the feeling of law to replace the thought of law" and which decried "the invasion of the force of instinct by the forces of a diabolical intellect."[203] Psychoanalytic theories, which belong to the postmodern mindset, even when they place lived experience at the heart of their clinical concerns, clearly do not involve a similar distrust of theory and do not necessarily consider emotional adherence to conceptual positions to be the criterion of validation. Nevertheless, they belong to a dominant current in which relativism and eclecticism, coupled with a pragmatism of effectiveness, offer little resistance to a cultural climate in which the criteria of the true and the good are becoming obsolete in thinking and in theoretical activity.

---

201 György Lukács.

202 Klemperer, *L.T.I.*

203 Ibid.

At the beginning of this chapter, we posed the question of why we should emphasize the rationalist aspects of Laplanche's theory as criteria of epistemological validation and as justification for preferring his theory to other psychoanalytic models. Laplanche's theorizing is grounded on a demand for truth, a demand that constitutes its motivating force.[204] It also constitutes its moral position. As Thomas Mann wrote, "The nasty, the stupid, and the false are equally bad, in other words, unworthy of man and disastrous."[205] Laplanche's theorizing involves a political component: Theories of knowledge, including psychoanalysis, are also a theories of society.[206] The lack of debate about the principal concepts of psychoanalysis and the assurance that they remain bearers of truth, even if they cover up realities whose differences and contradictions some seek to obscure, marks a troubling apolitical stance. Thomas Mann, who in 1918 had, with pride, published *Reflections of a Nonpolitical Man*, learned in spite of himself why this position was unacceptable and even dangerous. In 1939 he wrote, "One cannot escape politics. One only engages in them on the wrong side and with passion. To be apolitical is simply antidemocratic, which means that the mind, in suicidal manner, enters into conflict with all that is spiritual, this becomes clear only in certain extreme situations in which it appears in daylight and with great passion."[207]

Laplanche is deeply engaged in the debate about truth in psychoanalysis, including in his reading Freud's work and calling it into question. His theory is a committed theory, which embraces the work of systematization that his critical stance requires. The idea

---

204 Jean Laplanche, *The Unfinished Copernican Revolution* op. cit.

205 Thomas Mann, *L'artiste et la société*, trans. Louise Servicen (Paris: Grasset, 1973).

206 Christophe Dejours, "Psychanalyse et politique: Science, sexe et travail," *Filigrane* 8, no. 2 (1999): 6–20.

207 Thomas Mann, "Culture et politique," in *Les Maîtres*, trans. Louise Servicen and Jeanne Naujac (Paris: Grasset, 1979). [Translation modified.]

of a theoretical system is often mocked in contemporary culture—that is, when it is not simply discredited as the desire for mastery, as a totalitarianism of a thought that cannot deal with the anxiety of doubt or ambiguity. But the rigor of reflection is essential to democracy. Without making too much of the comparison of current cultural conditions and those that facilitated the rise of national socialism, let us recall the propositions Thomas Mann put in the mouth of the devil, the cultural embodiment of fascism in *Doctor Faustus*:[208] "We no longer acquire experience from the classical, my dear, but from the archaic, from the primitive. . . . Today, who knows any longer . . . the exaltation of the pure state of critique, of all paralyzing reflection, of all mortal control of reason? People say the devil is the spirit of critical disintegration.[209] It's another calumny, my friend. . . . If he is horrified by anything, if something offends him, it is critique, disintegrating critique. What he desires, what he provides, is precisely the triumphant projection beyond himself of brilliant lack of thought."[210210]

Brilliant lack of thought does not always take on the same form. This is why Laplanche's affiliation with the rationalist tradition constitutes a position of resistance, bearing the values of humanism that psychoanalysis should not forget.

---

208 Tessier (2007).

209 An allusion to the rationalism of Goethe, an antithetical figure of Nazism in German culture. In *Faust*, Mephistopheles says, "I am the spirit that always negates." 210 *Doctor Faustus* was finished in 1947.

210 Doctor Faustus was finished in 1947.

4

Rationalism and the From the Drive to Self-Knowledge Copernican Requirement:

Copernican decentering together with the resistance it encounters constitute through lines of Laplanche's close reading of Freud. What links is it reasonable to establish between the demands of Copernican decentering and rationalism?

We have seen that the primary character of the Copernican movement consists in situating the origin of the unconscious in the other, precisely in the other's messages compromised by the infantile sexual fantasies of the adults who take care of the child. This movement provides answers to questions that, in other psychoanalytic traditions, are either inadequately addressed or simply ignored: 1) How are sensory phenomena transformed into fantasy—that is, into psychic phenomena? 2) What is the origin of the content of fantasy? 3) How is nonsexual material transformed into sexual material? To confront these three questions constitutes a rationalist position: It implies a refusal of a leap into the irrational that these questions have previously occasioned.

Three other aspects of Laplanche's anthropology are representative of the connection of the demands of Copernicanism to the rationalist tradition, particularly in its dialectical dimension: the realism of the unconscious, the role of sexuality in the transition from consciousness to self-awareness, and finally, the conception of transformation, related to the psychic nature of the sexual unconscious and the translational hypothesis of repression. These three elements are related to different moments of rationalism. The realism of the unconscious, according to which what is first a message later takes on the characteristics of a thing, approaches the theme of reification as developed in Marxist theory. Moreover, the links established by the GTS between sexualization, humanization, and the formation of the ego evoke Hegel's thought about the transition from consciousness to self-awareness. As for the theory of translation that underlies the conception of transformation and transcendence in Laplanche's theoretical work, we find significant contributions both from classicism and from German romanticism. Insofar as this is owing to the thought of Goethe and Schiller,[211] it is a thought that notably exerted decisive influence on Hegel and Marx. Therefore, it will be useful, in order to refine our angle of approach to the philosophical tradition to which Laplanche's thinking relates, to return to our definition of rationalism.

1. Rationalism and Axiology: The Question of Truth

In addition to the three points that we have enumerated, one could undoubtedly identify other connections between Laplanche's thought and rationalism. Notably, we find references to René Descartes and Baruch Spinoza.[212] The thought of Jean Hyppolite, whose activity as a translator was fundamental, also clearly influenced Laplanche's work. Laplanche's style, the clarity of his thought, his use of irony, his handling of polemic, and his critical spirit place him in the lineage of French rationalism, especially that of Voltaire. These statements may seem impressionistic. One could object that Hegel and Jean Hyppolite are not entirely situated in the rationalist tradition and that in the end Marxist theory took an irrational turn—for example, in its positivist conception of the laws of history—and that the rationalism of the theory of translation of the German romantics is far from certain. One could also mention

---

211 Antoine Berman, *L'épreuve de l'étranger* (Paris: Gallimard, 1984).

212 These references are given by way of example and are not exhaustive.

the fact that Laplanche, although he described himself as "very rationalist and very Freudian,"[213] did not explicitly develop these points in his theorizing except perhaps by describing Freud, at the least the Freud of the demand [*de l'exigence*] of the unconscious, as a "wounded rationalist." Laplanche did, however, emphasize that the experience of the unconscious did not force psychoanalysis "to give up the rationalist option."[214] As for the Marxist inspiration for his work, Laplanche never claimed it. Even if FreudoMarxism— connected to the phylogenetic hypothesis—is not the Marxist reference that is mentioned in this book, one must nevertheless say clearly that Laplanche did not embrace it and in fact criticized its application to the understanding of social problems.[215] He rejected the idea of sexuality as an element of liberation and the idea of the unconscious as a factor in emancipation. Instead, Laplanche adopted Freud's position that psychoanalysis aims not to "liberate sexual life from all restraint" but "to free us from the yoke of the unconscious."[216] From this point of view, the idea of attributing a project of emancipation to psychoanalysis as theorized by Laplanche must be carefully examined. The concept is not explicit in Laplanche's theory. Rather, in this respect, he emphasizes Freud's caution, which Laplanche describes as a tactic, but he also considers it to be based on experience and the knowledge of the multiple factors, including psychic ones, that oppose emancipation of the individual.[217]

Here I am not seeking to link Laplanche's theorizing and Marxist thought as a political orientation or as favoring the

213 A. Luchetti, "Théorie de la seduction: validation et refutation," Psychiatrie française 38, no. 4 (December 2007): 148.

214 Jean Laplanche, *Freud and the Sexual* op cit

215 Jean Laplanche, *The Unfinished Copernican Revolution* op. cit.

216 Ibid., 78.

217 Ibid., 60.

reform of social structures. Nor am I seeking to relate Laplanche's theorizing to a specific philosophical theory. Rather, my aim is to explore Laplanche's thinking in relation to rationalism as defined in the preceding chapter. Above all, this involves a moral component. I take rationalism to be an epistemological category corresponding to a criterion of evaluation of theory, even of its validation. This criterion is not limited to the evaluation of psychoanalysis. On the contrary, the thesis I am arguing for is that rationalism constitutes a fundamental criterion for the validation of every theory in the human sciences. It is by sharing this common criterion that bridges can be established between psychoanalysis and other disciplines: It makes it possible to choose between theoretical orientations not only in psychoanalysis but also in the other disciplines. Indeed, it highlights the necessity for and the ethical aspects of these choices.

Rationalism, as we have defined it, implies a commitment to the search for truth. It also implies the conviction that this search for truth is a responsibility of reason. These statements are based on premises that are far from being unanimously accepted. They are grounded on positions of which the main three can be described as follows: 1) The assumption that, in the case of any specific proposition, truth exists and it is possible to search for it, without, of course, claiming that the truth is given from the outset or with certainty. 2) The affirmation that reason must renounce the "dodges" that accept as an ultimate explanation of human behavior assumptions that cannot be explained in terms of reason.[218] 3) The postulate, in the form of the "Nobility of the Spirit,"[219] of a dignity inherent in the human condition, embodied in its reflective dimension and its capacity to examine critically its own affects,

---

218 Albert Camus, *Le mythe de Sisyphe* (Paris: Gallimard, 1942).

219 This is the title that a French publisher gave to a collection of Thomas Mann's essays.

sensations, and motions, a dignity in which, "in man, nature and life are transcended: In man they lose their innocence; they receive the spirit—and the spirit is self-criticism."[220]

Thus, rationalism does not constitute a return to the body/soul opposition. Nor does it deny the dependence of the activities of the psyche on the body, which would be not only an irrationalist position but also irrational in itself.

In psychoanalysis, rationalism also aims to refute a vitalistic mysticism, which has cohabited with the mytho-symbolic orientation and its dogmatic aspects, a vitalism clearly present in certain AngloSaxon currents—for example, the transcendentalist influences in Winnicott's thinking and the more directly vitalistic influences in Bion's thinking.[221] In these currents a form of transcendence is associated with "the depths of the flesh" whose "epiphenomenon is the affectivity manifested as in feelings."[222] [222]This position is problematic, not because of the emphasis it places on affect as experienced nor because of The temporal priority it gives to the influence of bodily excitation on the phenomena of the soul.[223] Problems arise because it supposes that sensations are correlative to primordial meanings, to contents prior to the capacity to synthesize those contents, to signification prior to meaning. From this point of view, what is created is fertile ground for the growth of belief in the mytho-symbolic.[224] In addition to the jump

---

220 Thomas Mann, "La philosophie de Nietzsche à la lumière de notre experience," in *Les Maîtres*, 249.

221 The relationship among these tendencies and the links between pragmatism and Bergson's philosophy should be examined from this perspective. Hélène Tessier, *La psychanalyse americaine* (Paris: Presses Universitaires de France, 2005).

222 B. Borgo, "Chair métaphysique, chaire de force: Lévinas face à Nietzsche," *Europe: revue littéraire mensuelle* 89, nos. 991–92 (November–December 2011).

223 Laplanche, *The Unfinished Copernican Revolution*

224 E. Gentile, *Qu'est-ce que le fascisme?: Histoire et interprétation*, trans. P.-E. Dauzat (Paris: Gallimard, 2004).

into the irrational, there are potential dangers on the moral level because this position situates transcendence within life and, as a result, puts it "beyond good and evil." Thus, the philosophies of life, the thought of Nietzsche, and specifically Bergsonian vitalism in its relations with pragmatism played a determining role in Mussolini's fascism.[225] These developments have been described in the works of Thomas Mann and Victor Klemperer.[226] In his 1947 essay on Nietzsche,[227] Thomas Mann comments with anxiety on the idea that, apart from life, there would be no fixed point from which to reflect on existence, "no authority before which life could be ashamed." "Really?" he wrote. "One has the feeling that there is such an authority nevertheless—granted that it is not morality—it is simply the human spirit, humanity itself that is critical, irony and freedom united with the verb that judges."[228]

In the essay written for Freud's birthday in 1936, Thomas Mann denounced the overvaluation of the sensory, intuitive, and vital phenomena, which, according to him, Freudian theory had resisted.[229] Such an overvaluation, corresponding to the primacy of the vital, was rooted in romantic thought and in his view could be explained, notably in Nietzsche, by the search for a "corrective against a certain saturation by rationalism." This search was

---

225 György Lukács, and Gentile, *Qu'est-ce que le fascisme?*.

226 Klemperer, commenting on the philosophy of Martin Buber, shows how the tendency to place "mysticism above rationalism" is rooted in the romanticism that prevailed at the time, and from that well "is drawn the water of one against the other, of the innocent and the poisoners, of the victims and the torturers." *L.T.I.: La langue du IIIe Reich*, trans. E. Guillot (Paris: Albin Michel, 1996), 277–78.

227 Thomas Mann, "La philosophie de Nietzsche à la lumière de notre expérience," in *Les Maîtres*.

228 Ibid.

229 This explained, according to Thomas Mann, the antipathy it had aroused in "the drunken spirit of the mysticism of the unconscious," in this case Nazism. This text follows the book burnings of 1933, which included Freud's books.

based on false premises revealing a "total lack of knowledge . . . of the balance of power between instinct (Instinkt) and intellect on earth." Mann observed the disastrous proportions taken on by what initially had been only a cultural movement. Thomas Mann believed that rectification of this error was a moral duty: "When one thinks of how much, in the majority of humans, will, drive [*der Trieb*], and interest dominate and crush intellect, reason, and the sense of right, the notion that intellect must be overcome by instinct becomes an absurdity. . . . As if it were really necessary to defend life against the psyche! As if there were the slightest danger that the mind could reign too much on earth! The simplest nobility of the heart should compel us to keep and protect the meager little flame of reason, of spirit, of justice."[230]

The anthropology of Laplanche arises from the same convictions. The GTS is not a theory of the intellect, nor is it a theory of the mind. It is a psychoanalytic theory and consequently a theory of the soul, which focuses on one of the soul's specific aspects, the sexual unconscious. To avoid the confusion between the sexual unconscious and other aspects of sexuality, Laplanche uses the term "*sexual*," a neologism in French. In the 2007 introduction to *Freud and the Sexual* he writes:

> [B]y using ["sexual,"] this slightly strange term, which is, nevertheless, extracted from Freud, I have sought to affirm the primacy within psychoanalysis of a unique and specific 'variety' of sexuality. It is this that is at the heart of the notions of the drive, the unconscious, and even the "death drive": the sexuality that, at least in infancy, can transform any region or function of the body, and even activity in general, into an "erotogenic zone."

---

230 Mann, "La philosophie de Nietzsche à la lumière de notre expérience," 249–50.

It would, however, be one-sided to reduce this enlarged sexuality to the polymorphous perverse sexuality of early childhood. This anarchic sexuality,
whose fate is sometimes close to the "sexual death
drive," has another, more stabilizing fate and one
to which Freud attached the name "renunciation of
the drive." The path of renunciation is not purely
negative. It is the path of binding within the field of
genitality and, more generally, the path of sublimation. This is what Freud calls "the Eros of the divine
Plato," and it is no less erotic for all that. . . . It is
essential that this fate, which is by no means always
conformist, not be forgotten.[231]

His anthropology examines the origin of the sexual unconscious
and its role in the process of humanization. It carves out strict
limits for the epistemological field of psychoanalysis. As we have
recalled, it looks for "the process occurring in a previously living
being starting from the moment when a sexual unconscious comes
to exist."[232]

The question of rationalism does not arise in relation to the object
of psychoanalysis itself. It arises in relation to the way in which
one accounts for its origin, for its mode of action, for its relations
with the body, with other components of the soul, and with other
faculties of the mind. In this respect, Laplanche's theorizing remains
far removed from a "mysticism of the unconscious" and equally
far removed from mythologizing sexuality. His anthropology is a
humanist anthropology whose fundamental axis, which is the same
axis as he ascribes to analytic treatment, consists of "an unshakable

---

231 Jean Laplanche, *Freud and the Sexual* (New York: Unconscious in Translation,
2011), 2.
232 Jean Laplanche, "The Unfinished Copernican Revolution," op. cit.

trust in the power of truth."[233] The transformative role of truth manifests itself especially in the relations between the unconscious and the alterity, as they are described in the GTS.

2. From the External to the Internal Otherness: *Afflavit   et Dissipati Sunt*

Afflavit et dissipati sunt,[234] an expression quoted by Freud in *The Interpretation of Dreams* on the occasion of the interpretation of one of his dreams, is an allusion to the inscription on an English coin commemorating the annihilation of the Spanish Armada. Laplanche takes it up in his paper "Must We Burn Melanie Klein?"[235] He emphasizes that Freud's rationalism is related "to 'Enlightenment' philosophy: . . . There where reason comes to light, nocturnal demons disappear forever."[236] In his diary of 1934, while expressing deep concerns about the rise of Nazism and the slave mentality that it favors, Klemperer quotes the same motto. He asks himself: "In their fight against mind, against whom will the Hitlerians fail?" And he replies: "*Deus afflabit,*[237] but when?"[238]

In these passages, Laplanche and Klemperer both evoke rationalism and both appeal to the supernatural and to the demonic, that demonic element, *Lucifer amor*, already described in the preceding chapters. Laplanche's "nocturnal demons" refers to dreams but also to the sexual unconscious. Klemperer does not refer directly to the demons—rather to their antithesis, to God—

---

233 Jean Laplanche, "Defence and Prohibition in Treatment and in the Psychoanalytic Account of the Human," op. cit.

234 "There was a breath (of wind) and they disappeared."

235 Jean Laplanche, "Should We Burn Melanie Klein?" op. cit.

236 Ibid.

237 *Afflabit* is the future tense.

238 Victor Klemperer, *Mes soldats de papier: Journal 1933–1941*, trans. G. Riccardi (Paris: Seuil, 2000), 150.

but at the moment of invoking this quote, he is focusing on "the encouragement of vices typical of slaves."[239] Is there a connection between the theme of slavery and that of the demonic?

As we have explained in chapter 2, one of the major contributions of the GTS to the social sciences consists in the explanation that it provides for the "psychic springs of voluntary servitude."[240] It clarifies consenting to and collaborating with domination, in the sense described by La Boétie. In a given society, it is not only a matter of a "relationship of domination/servitude" but most important of a relationship that is tied to "the most intimate aspects of consciousness."[241] The originary position that the GTS confers on masochism is a decisive contribution to the analysis of this question. To the extent that masochism constitutes a dimension that is not only fundamental to human sexuality but also its first dimension, it is not surprising that the attraction to submission, the fascination with power, with hierarchy and its symbols, even with the "sacralization" of domination,[242] are characteristic of human behavior. That is why we formulated the hypothesis that drive renunciation is not so much aimed at sexual desires, as generally understood, but rather aimed at renunciation of masochistic satisfaction, satisfaction on which various social systems, including the family, all too often rely in order to remain effective and ensure their authority. Laplanche has emphasized this aspect of drive renunciation by defining sublimation as "the transposition of the sexual drives of death into the energy of the sexual drives of life."[243]

---

239 Ibid.

240 Christophe Dejours, *Conjurer la violence* (Paris: Payot, 2007).

241 J.-P. Auffret, in É. La Boétie, *Discours sur la servitude volontaire* (Paris: Mille et une nuits, 1995).

242 Gentile, *Qu'est-ce que le fascisme?*

243 Jean Laplanche, "Sublimation and/or Inspiration," in *Between Seduction and Inspiration: Man.*

In that definition he is clarifying his conception of drive renunciation as one of the two possible fates for the *sexual*, the other fate being to come closer to the sexual drive of death. Drive renunciation, he writes, is "by no means always conformist":[244] Conformism actually represents a form of linkage to masochism or sadomasochism. Drive renunciation, as a distancing from masochistic satisfaction, makes possible the resistance and opposition to received wisdom and so "exerts a liberatory effect on the soul," offering an opening to "a better, more beautiful, more equitable life according to the spirit."[245]

Laplanche's article on Klein[246] begins with the evocation of nocturnal demons and of *"dissipati sunt"* and ends with a reference to Hegel: to the "struggle to death of consciences" and to the "masterslave dialectic," to which we will return. For the moment let us use this reference to comment on one aspect of Laplanche's theory of the drive: the passage of a message from the adult, the external other, to the child's internal other, the unconscious thing, the untranslated residue of the adult's message, the "designated signifier."[247] The reference to Hegel in the article on Klein is found at the moment when Laplanche evokes the theme of spirits and ghosts: "What Hegel did not see is that there is no fight to death that does not bring back ghosts."[248] This allusion, which links in a logical sequence the sexual unconscious (nocturnal demons), the birth of the drive (the fight to the death of consciences),[249] and

---

244 Laplanche, *Freud and the Sexual*.

245 Thomas Mann, "Essai sur Tchekhov," in *Erika Mann: La dernière année*, trans. Louise Servicen (Paris: Gallimard, 1967), 209.

246 Laplanche, " Should We Burn Melanie Klein?", op. cit.

247 Cf. Jean Laplanche, "A Brief Treatise on the Unconscious," in *Between Seduction and Inspiration: Man*.

248 Laplanche, "Should We Burn Melanie Klein?," op. cit.

249 This point is developed in the following section.

ghosts, constitutes a good introduction to the concept of the realism of the unconscious, especially as it has striking similarities with the Marxist theory of reification that is closely related to the conception of transformation that underlies the GTS.

a) The Historical Otherness of the Unconscious "Thing": From a Human Relationship to a Relationship with a Thing

Let's go back a bit to summarize the sequence proposed by the GTS. It postulates that the origin of the sexual unconscious lies in the unconscious sexual fantasies of the adult who takes care of the child. These fantasies compromise the messages—verbal and nonverbal—that the adult addresses to the child and that, at this stage, are at first implanted in the "psychophysiological skin" of the child. This first inscription of the adult's messages "does not require translation . . . the messages are perceptual phenomena that 'make a sign to' the child—that is, they 'signal' that they are addressed to the child. They do not need to be translated into signifiers of; they are immediately registered as *signifiers to*."[250] In a second stage, the trauma of this break-in from the external other becomes self-traumatization and causes repression: "[I]t is at the level of temporalization conceived as a narrativization, a translation of enigmas emanating from the other, and then of an ongoing 'self-theorization,' that repression is to be situated—precisely as a failure of that temporalization and as a deposition of untranslated residues."[251]

This process shows why the sexual unconscious has the characteristics of a thing: It is the result of a failure of temporalization; it is timeless. Moreover, having lost all reference to meaning, it is not affected by negation or contradiction, which are logical categories,

---

250 Laplanche, "Brief Treatise on the Unconscious," 86.
251 Ibid., 92.

categories of meaning. Like a thing, the unconscious manifests itself in ways that do not involve communicative intent.[252] As a result, drive energy is distinguished by its unbound nature. Laplanche separates himself from Freud's physicalist framework and defines this energy in terms of the translational model: Unbound energy consists of a "circulation of nonsense."[253] Meaning is what links affect to representation. The sexual drive attacks this link. As Laplanche puts it, "The reasons for that unbinding, and for the primary process governing the unconscious contents, are to be sought nowhere else than in repression itself, [which breaks] connections between the elements of the message and, above all, disconnects the link between signifier and signified. The unconscious contents are the residue of that strange metabolism,[254] which 'treats' the messages of the other but fails to 'treat' the strangeness itself. It is those 'designified signifiers' that pursue their existence side by side in the unconscious, or contract between them the most absurd alliances (i.e., by displacement-condensation)."[255] On the side of the ego, a network for the circulation of meaning is created. Thus psychic conflict is a conflict of drives, a conflict "between sexual drives of death" (sexuality in its most unleashed form) and "the sexual drives of life" (drives oriented toward totality, toward synthesis); it is "a conflict between the two agencies, the ego as a center of binding, dominated by Eros, and the id where there are various degrees of unbinding, going as far as the sexual death drive that is

252 Jean Laplanche, "Goals of the Psychoanalytic Process," in *Between Seduction and Inspiration: Man*, 195.

253 Jean Laplanche, "The Drive and Its Source-Object," op. cit.

254 By the term "metabolism," Laplanche refers to linguistic processes. See Jean Laplanche, "Forces at Play in Psychical Conflict," in *Between Seduction and Inspiration: Man*, 117n172, and Jean Laplanche, *The Unconscious and the Id*, trans. Luke Thurston and Lindsey Watson (London: Rebus, 1999), 112–13.

255 Laplanche, "Forces at Play in Psychical Conflict," 127.

the id's central abyss."[256]

The sexual unconscious, "the empire of the unbound,"[257] presents itself as a "pure culture" or even a "quintessence of otherness."[258] It comes from a dual source: It is "Copernican"—as it comes from the other—and thinglike. Laplanche writes: "Through the process of repression, psychical alterity has radically changed place: In the initial Copernican relation, it is the relationship to the other person—*der Andere*—that is at stake. Once the psychical system closes in on itself, with the constitution of the ego as an agency, the alterity or otherness became internal: The id becomes *das Andere*, the other par excellence, but an internal other."[259] He also writes that the unconscious "is the other thing (*das Andere*) in me, the repressed residue of the other person (*der Andere*). It affects me, just as the other person once affected me in the past."[260]

This description of a relationship that is first and foremost a relation of human communication, from which the individual subsequently creates the experience of a relation to a thing, evokes Marxist thought about reification. Such a frame of reference makes it possible to understand the importance that Laplanche gives to the category of cause and the care he puts into demonstrating the causal

256 Laplanche, "Goals of the Psychoanalytic Process," 194.

257 Jean Laplanche, *Between Seduction and Inspiration: Man*, trans. Jeffrey Mehlman (New York: Unconscious in Translation, 2015), 82.

258 Ibid., 115. Quintessence (*quinta ssential*): ether, the fifth body of ancient philosophy, from which the soul is made. Laplanche is alluding to the philosophy of Aristotle, in connection with the "first immobile mover," another pillar of Aristotelian cosmology, an expression that Laplanche uses to describe the fundamental anthropological situation. Ether would also be the element in which this first immobile mover is located.

259 Ibid., 194.

260 Ibid. And here is another, older passage on the same theme: "[T]he other thing (*das Andere*) that is the unconscious is maintained in its radical alterity only by the other person (*der Andere*): in brief, by seduction." Laplanche, "Unfinished Copernican Revolution" op. cit.

relationship that links the unconscious with human behavior.

b) The Reification

The theory of reification is a theory of alienation. Nevertheless, alienation must not be conflated with objectification. In Marxist theory, the recognition of a reality independent of subjective consciousness is not alienation.[261] The suppression of alienation is not a matter of overcoming objectivity. Objectivity is neither good nor bad: Liberation is just as objective as servitude. Alienation as a social relation occurs only when, in society, objective forms assume aspects that "oppress, torment, and disfigure the essence of man."[262] In other words, when the representation these forms give social relations disguises them and so describes a false reality or pseudoreality.

In Marxist thought, it is reification flowing from the market as a social formation that constitutes the form of alienation. Private property, Marx wrote, is "the sensible expression of the fact that man becomes both objective for himself and a nonhuman object alien to himself."[263] Here we can observe a connection with Laplanche's theory of the formation of the sexual unconscious, in which a relation, first of all a human relation, becomes a relation with a thing. Before we continue the comparison between the theory of reification and the GTS, it is important to prevent a possible misunderstanding. The Marxist theory of reification is a critique of the deception established as a social formation by the market,

261 This is notably in contrast to alienation in existentialist theories in which alienation begins with an insurmountable distance between subject and object. Moreover, in Lukács's view, in Hegel's theorizing objectification and alienation are inseparable. See György Lukács, *Histoire et conscience de classe*, trans. K. Axelos and J. Bois (Paris: Minuit, 1960).

262 Lukács, *Histoire et conscience de classe*.

263 Karl Marx, *Philosophie*, ed. M. Rubel (Paris: Gallimard, 1994), 151.

a deception inherent in the relation between the worker and the fruits of his labor. The comparison made with Laplanche's theory does not deal with this deception. Moreover, although it would be possible to make such a case, the comparison itself does not argue that Laplanche's theory involves a critique of the market form. The goal here is different. It aims to draw a parallel between the GTS and the Marxist theory of alienation to highlight the rationalist features of the two theories. The theory of reification is a rationalist theory. It refuses to accept the empirical real as an impenetrable given and does not limit itself to a partial system of thought from which an abstract conception of reality would flow. It is shaped by a demand for truth that aims to unmask what is hidden behind the observable. It tends toward the transformation of reality. The GTS shares these characteristics. The purpose of the comparison with Marxist theory is to show the role played by the transformation of a human relation into a relation with a thing, since both of these theories places this at the center of their conception of alienation. This comparison also makes it possible to highlight the systematic character of Laplanche's theory and the importance of each of its components within the whole.

With this clarification established, let us return to the theory of reification. It implies that humans no longer see property, the products of labor, and the means of production, for what they are: the instantiation of social and interhuman activities. Instead they regard them as objects that are external;[264] they take the social character of their own work as its natural property.[265] Thus, it is "the socially determined relationship between men that appears to

---

264 In the current economic context, we could add that the market itself appears as a fact of nature.

265 Marx, *Philosophie*.

men in the phantasmagorical form of a relation of things."[266] This quote from Lukács echoes the GTS. The connection is even more striking if we stop at the term "phantasmagoria," which refers to the ghosts *"dissipati sunt"* to whom Laplanche refers in his text on Melanie Klein—a text where, incidentally, the vocabulary of witchcraft is preponderant. Laplanche gives the rationalist aspect of the *"dissipati sunt"* concrete form.

Moreover, in Marxist theory, the phenomenon of reification, which is first considered in connection with specific categories of activity, is later extended to all consciousness: It compromises[267] the whole of the apprehension of reality. The GTS describes a similar situation: Originally, reification concerns part of a message whose form of being becomes general in the constitution of the child's sexual unconscious and in the resulting psychical conflicts. Eventually it invades the whole of the life of the soul.

Another convergence between the two theories can be seen in the description of the mercantile form of being and the description of the sexual unconscious—namely, the loss of reference to meaning and the resulting interchangeability of content. The characteristics of the contents of the unconscious correspond to the characteristics of things: timelessness, absence of negation, and inexistence of contradiction. Laplanche emphasizes that these characteristics are not given, not innate, but rather the result of repression.[268] The absence of a signifying intention, the absence of negation, and the absence of contradiction are consequences of the transformation of

---

266 Lukács, *Histoire et conscience de classe,* 114.

267 [Translator's note: Here the notion of "compromise" can be understood precisely in the Freudian sense, in the same sense as Laplanche uses the concept when speaking of the adult's sexual unconscious as compromising the adult's attachment communications with the infans.]

268 Reification that has also been at work in the adult and that results in the compromised part of its message.

the content of a message into a thing. The associative/dissociative method [which, as Laplanche points out, would be a more accurate term than free association] relies on this thing like character of the derivatives of the unconscious to trace their historical course. To this end, it resorts to metonymy but especially to homonymy, which together constitute current interpretative procedures: "Homonymy designates two words pronounced [or even written] identically and having no relation of derivation between them, having different histories and contexts and often having different etymologies."[269] The use of homonymy in psychoanalytic interpretations relies on the mutual permutability of words whose meaning is not equivalent, but which are interchangeable insofar as they are truly "words [or signifiers] taken for things."[270]

This aspect can, *mutatis mutandis*, be compared with the Marxist theory in which one of the main consequences of reification consists in the "permutability of qualitatively different objects," made possible by the transformation of social relations into commodities. This parallel illustrates how the rationalist attachment of the GTS is inseparable from the category of the message. Indeed, without message, there is neither interhuman communication nor reification, and without reification there is no way to account for the loss of reference to meaning. In this case, there would also be no valid explanation for making the associative/dissociative method a privileged mode of access to the derivatives of the unconscious.

Two other elements allow us to deepen the connections between the Marxist theory of reification and the GTS. The first deals with the relationship between theorization and alienation and the second with the consequences for psychoanalytic theory of understanding reification.

---

269 Laplanche, "Brief Treatise on the Unconscious," 97n122.
270 Ibid., 94.

Alienation and Theorization

As much in Marxist theory as in psychoanalysis, the rationalist position consists in combating the myth, often associated with rationality, according to which we can recognize ourselves only in our conscious acts. Marxist theory has criticized such a position: The market form constitutes a form of irrationality. Psychoanalytic theory moves in the same direction: The ego is not master in its own home. A rationality based on intentionality, needs, and conscious motivation alone cannot account for human behavior. In the GTS, the "other," which "acts" according to own logic, is described as the "unconscious thing." The duty of understanding consists in bringing to light the true origin of this relation to things, not in mystifying or poeticizing or ignoring it. It is also a question of revealing its alienated character not only because it holds a real grip on subjectivity but also because the origin attributed to it is false. In Marxist theory, the relation of things appears to the worker as a superhuman reality, which cannot be changed and over which the worker has no power. The scientific theories that transmit this false reality participate in creating alienation and reinforcing it.[271] Laplanche's scientific approach consists in a historical deconstruction of the thing-like character of the unconscious, and in this way the entirely human origin of the unconscious is revealed. On this subject, important clarifications are necessary.

It is necessary to distinguish the alienation resulting from the process of reification and the alienation coming from theory, which is itself a product of reification. The sexual unconscious is not pathological: It is one of the necessary conditions of becoming human, of emancipation of the living toward the sphere of humanity. The aim of psychoanalysis summed up by the formula "*Wo Es war, sol Ich werden*" implies a liberation from "the compulsions of

271 Lukács, *Histoire et conscience de classe.*

fantasy"[272] and thus, for the individual, a greater range for freedom of choice. The alienation described by the GTS operates in the relation between the individual and his own unconscious. But this state of alienation is in fact reinforced by psychoanalytic theories either when the process of reification is obscured or when its historical, interhuman origins are denied or ignored by attributing a genetic origin to the unconscious (primal fantasies, phylogenesis). This is why the demand for a "Copernican" understanding occupies a central place in Laplanche's theory.

The tendency of theory to close up the subject on itself constitutes an effect of reification. It is doubly alienating since the very stage of reification is denied. If the origin of the unconscious is not at first in an activity of interpersonal communication and does not entail the transformation of part of the message into a thing, there is no reification. Two possibilities arise. Either, (1) as traditional psychoanalysis has thought, the "thing" already exists in culture, before the existence of the individual, and thus it acts as a natural phenomenon in all humans; its action is inescapable, universal, and immutable—its transmission takes place either by phylogenesis or by already reified structures. Or, alternatively, (2) there is no reification, because fantasies take root in an intersubjective relational framework where they are immediately associated with affect, with experience, with subjectivity, and do not include noncommunicative "foreign bodies" presented to the subject in the character of things. In this case, everything happens on the human level, that is to say, on the subjective level. There is no reification. Without prior alienation, no disalienation; a thought process leading to disalienation must include a thought of alienation: "[I] n refusing to recognize in ourselves a foreign body as hard as iron,

---

272 Jean Laplanche, "The So-called Death Drive: A Sexual Drive," in *Between Seduction and Inspiration: Man*, 170.

'disalienating' thought deprives itself of the path leading from the other-thing in us to the other person that is its origin. It fails in this to discover that the internal alienation is the residue of a fundamental decentering whose center is the adult other for the child, whose gravitational pull is to be situated in the enigmatic message."[273]

Reification, and consequently alienation, entails the transformation of a social relation, that is to say, a relation between humans, in connection with a thing stripped of its human characteristics. This concept lies at the foundation of the GTS. The sexual unconscious is not endowed with a natural or hereditary origin. "The drive," writes Laplanche, "is not originally a 'natural' reality but a true 'second nature' deposited in man through the effects of the child's relation to the adult socius."[274]

The Contribution of the Theory of Reification: The Connection between Causality and Fantasy

Locating the origin of the drive in the other has consequences for understanding the stakes of psychic conflict and the process of transformation. Indeed, if the origin of the drive were a "natural" reality, its action would be governed by laws, since laws govern natural phenomena. In psychoanalytic theorizing that adopts a phylogenetic account of the origin of the drive, the drives original content is myth, myth derived from an ahistorical and thus naturalized culture. This "naturalized origin" of the drive joins "the biologizing wandering astray of sexuality."[275] Relational and intersubjectivist currents, which consider psychical processes as subjective productions, do not refer to the notion of law.

273 Laplanche, "Brief Treatise on the Unconscious," 92. [Translation modified.]

274 Laplanche, "So-called Death Drive: A Sexual Drive," 178n229.

275 See Jean Laplanche, *The Temptation of Biology: Freud's Theories of Sexuality* the English, trans. Donald Nicholson-Smith (New York: Unconscious in Translation, 2015).

Paradoxically, they are dependent on a form of law in adopting a psychological conception of the life of the soul, especially regarding psychopathology. Here the notion of the psychological is to be understood not as opposed to the biological but, on the contrary, as a domain within biology (ethology, developmental psychology, psychology of learning, etc.). This is why attachment theory, in which the notion of law asserts itself, plays a major role and the connections with the cognitive sciences are so easily made.

Marxist theory has established a tight link between the reification of consciousness and that conception of society according to which society changes according to universal laws that are independent of human activity. Citing Marx, Lukács sums up the effect of reification in this way: Social relations appear to humans as a second nature, governed by laws.[276] "For humans, their own social movement takes on the form of a movement of things that control them instead of being controlled by them."[277]

In the same way, for psychoanalysis, Laplanche insists on the importance of recognizing that the relations between the unconscious and human thoughts and behaviors are not governed by laws, although the temptation to refer to this category may be strong because, in its unbound aspect—as a reified entity—the unconscious seems to act without the intervention of the subject. The alternative understanding that Laplanche proposes adopts the category of cause, a category linked to a historical perspective on transformation.

—The Category of Cause

Causality has a temporal dimension. It entails a historical sequence

---

276 Note the similarity of vocabulary with Laplanche's text quoted above, which describes the drive as a "second nature."

277 Lukács, *Histoire et conscience de classe.*

that starts from the present and turns to the past to apprehend the future. "Becoming," writes Lukács, "is a mediation between the past and the future."[278] This conception of temporality constitutes another element of the parallel between the GTS and the historical dialectic, since, according to Laplanche, the axis present-past-future constitutes the axis of psychoanalytic temporality. This axis is tightly linked to the category of the message and owes a great deal to the temporality of the translation. "From its beginning, psychoanalysis has privileged a turning to the past from the moment of the present. We are left with the task of interpreting the sequence present-pastfuture in the light of a detranslation/retranslation theory of human existence and of connecting this movement, which itself gives rise to diachrony, back to the synchronic driving force that is the originary situation of seduction."[279]

Cause is not a predictive category. As Laplanche writes, "Causality is not a law. It does not establish constant relations between phenomena, but it achieves its effects almost magically or mechanically. In this sense, it has indeed been dethroned from all sciences, including history, in favor of correlations that may take the form of a function. However, I would like to suggest that with psychoanalysis, the old-fashioned cause, the archaic cause, has found its true homeland, in the deep sense where metapsychology is the *repatriation* of the metaphysical."[280]

Laplanche specifies that [in terms of the Aristotelian opposition between final and material causes] the causal modalities that apply

---

278 Lukács, *Histoire et conscience de classe.*

279 Jean Laplanche, "Temporality and Translation," op. cit.

280 Jean Laplanche, "Interpretation Between Determinism and Hermeneutics: a New Approach to the Problem op. cit. This is an allusion to *Psychopathology of Everyday Life*, in which Freud writes: "One could venture to explain in this way the myths of paradise and the fall of man, of God, of good and evil, of immortality, and so on, and to transform metaphysics into metapsychology."

to the unconscious are not final but rather material causes.[281] The contents of the unconscious, "the designified signifiers," partly furnish the material that constitutes the more or less connected representations that are formed in the unconscious and the ego. The representations are, in turn, causally related to thoughts and actions. That is why we can say that repression gives rise to a "certain type of reality, called unconscious,"[282] a reality that then infiltrates all human reality.

This aspect constitutes another element of the possible parallel between the GTS and the theory of reification. The latter also accounts for the formation of a type of reality that operates in all spheres of thought. The question presented both by unconscious reality and by reified reality is the question of their relationship to the truth. In a reified consciousness, truth can be presented only in reified form. Neither the search for truth nor its definition can avoid reification. How would they escape it? Similarly, what is the relation of unconscious reality to truth? In both theories, the answer to this question runs through two closely related elements. On the one hand, it involves repositioning reification as a moment in a process rather than as a raw fact; on the other hand, it involves practice as necessary for disalienation. We will, briefly, examine these two elements.

—Fantasizing and Disalienation: Reification as a Process

The category of the cause implies that the unconscious does not constitute a "primal" entity: It is the made up of the untranslated residues of a process of translation. The loss of reference that affects its content and gives it the character of a thing constitutes a moment of that process.

---

281 Laplanche, "Temporality and Translation," 403n2.
282 Laplanche, "Brief Treatise on the Unconscious," 66.

Although it is an alienated reality, the psychic reality that repressed content contributes to creating is nonetheless an actual reality. It is illusory to think that a given individual could have access to any material or historical reality independent of his psychic reality. Moreover, the fact that psychic reality may be the only effective reality for a given individual does not mean there is no other reality independent of the indisputable effects of the individual's psychic reality. The problem of the relation of alienated consciousness to the truth evokes Aristotle's degrees of being: *"Veritas est id, quod est"* — the truth is what is.[283] But what is? As Marx has observed, "Did not the old Moloch reign? Was not the Apollo of Delphi a real power in the life of the Greeks?"

Parallel to how Marxist theory accounts for the reified reality of the market, the GTS accounts for the ontological difference between psychic reality and reality. In psychic reality, ultimately the core of fantasy is linked to the sexual drive of death, in fact to nonbeing. By recognizing the reification of repressed contents as a moment in the formation process of the unconscious, while reaffirming the essentially human origin of these contents, the GTS makes it possible to affirm the preponderant role of psychic reality, without giving it the status of unique or suprareal reality. It also makes it possible to define psychic reality for what it is: a reified reality. To return to the theme of the ghost, one could say that instead of the fantasy of a relationship of things, the GTS makes the "too human" human appear, the human who is profiled behind the blind and inexorable force of the "unconscious thing." The ghost vanishes, giving way to the harsh reality of relationships between humans. As Albert Camus wrote in *The Myth of Sisyphus*: It "makes destiny a human question that must be settled by humans."

---

283 I. Schüssler, *La question de la vérité* (Lausanne: Payot, PhiloGenos, 1982).

—Practice

Going backward along the path leading from the other of the message to the unconscious thing makes it possible to deconstruct the process of reification. The feeling of being acted upon by obscure forces loses its natural—or supernatural—and immutable character. In the Marxist theory of reification, finding the social—the interhuman—relationship behind what takes the form of a thing calls into question the ineluctable character of the existing order. For instance, while the idea that "capital produces fruits as the pear tree produces pears" constitutes a proposition that is acceptable, even indisputable, for a reified consciousness. By showing the human origin of capital accumulation, by demonstrating that it results from social relations established and maintained by humans, this proposition reveals the situation as subject to change.

The recognition of the human origin of the unconscious, as such recognition does for other reified entities, makes it possible to highlight its historical character: What is created or instituted by humans is neither innate nor natural. If relationships between humans are historical, they are also transformable: What comes from human relationships can be modified by humans.

In Marxist theory, the conditions of possibility of such modification exist in practice. Similarly, for Laplanche "the theory of seduction is not a 'language' to be read but an effort to understand analytic practice."[284] This sets up a situation that does not merely bring into play forces already present in the psychic conflict. The psychoanalytic situation that provokes transference "is an attempt to put the primal process back on track, a process in which the other 'to be conquered' was not the unconscious internal other but the external other as source of enigmatic messages. That other was, in

---

284 Laplanche, "Brief Treatise on the Unconscious," 89n138.

earlier times, the origin of a genuine 'drive to translate.'"[285]

Other situations may also set in motion a process whose outcome attenuates the influence of internal otherness in favor of a new relationship with external otherness; at least one hopes so. In this respect Laplanche invokes mourning,[286] and Dejours[287] invokes work. Involving the other not only as a source but also as a recipient of the message makes these occasions of "inspiration," a concept Laplanche uses to redefine sublimation. With this, he is evoking G. W. F. Hegel and Friedrich Hölderlin, recalling that "the source of inspiration is nothing but the object of the quest."[288] From this perspective, otherness truly becomes "an other to conquer." Like Goethe's Faust, the individual can open up more constructively to humanity.

3. Sexuality and Reflexivity: From Consciousness to Self-Awareness

The primacy of the other in the constitution of the unconscious makes it possible to situate the reification of the contents of the unconscious in a historical perspective. Can we take the historicity of the human subject, in this case the ability to fit itself into a story, as a given? This question, insofar as it belongs to the epistemology of psychoanalysis, amounts to asking whether there is a link between temporalization and the formation of the sexual unconscious.

Laplanche has devoted several texts to the questions of time, temporalization, and history. As we saw in chapter 2, he describes the ego as an "agency that temporalizes itself," as opposed to the unconscious fantasy that, in its hard core, remains fixed, ahistorical,

---

285 Laplanche, "Goals of the Psychoanalytic Process," 199.

286 Jean Laplanche, *The Unfinished Copernican Revolution* op. cit.

287 Christophe Dejours, *Travail vivant* (Paris: Payot, 2009).

288 Laplanche, *Temptation of Biology*, 7.

and immutable. Temporalization and the ability to be historicized are related to meaning. Since the ego, an entity that tends toward meaningful binding, owes its constitution to repression and that repression is concomitant with the formation of the sexual unconscious, there is thus a link between temporalization, repression, and the sexual unconscious.

Established by the GTS, the relationships between temporalization and the sexual unconscious are particularly important to understanding the primal position of masochism in sexuality. Masochism is linked to a specific moment in the temporalization of the drive that Laplanche called the "auto-moment," the time of autoeroticism, defined as "a series of founding moments in which unconscious fantasy and the excitement linked to (the 'drive') are in a single process (that of repression). The excitation, too, is necessarily experienced in a masochistic way as a painful assault of an *internal foreign body*, in relation to which the ego is passive."[289] As we have already said, this "auto-moment," which seals the primal position of masochism in human sexuality, is evocative of the dialectic domination/servitude,[290] which, in Hegel's *The Phenomenology of Mind*, illustrates the consequences of the transition from consciousness to self-awareness. The symbolism of domination/ servitude, or master/slave, is linked to masochistic fantasies, in the ordinary meaning of "masochistic," which is why the parallel between the primal position of masochism and the master/slave dialectic is so striking.

Some aspects of Hegel's thought are relevant to a better understanding of the concepts of the GTS, as well as its rationalist

---

289 Jean Laplanche, "Masochism and the General Theory of Seduction," op. cit. 533

290 "Domination/servitude" is the expression adopted by J. Hyppolite in the title of the section presenting this dialectic. (1941/1999), 1:155. In this text, I use the expression *master / slave* which is the form used by Laplanche.

postulates. The master/slave dialectic, and its position in the transition from "dependent" consciousness to "independent" consciousness, is one of these postulates. Without discussing Hegel's relation to the rationalist tradition, we will examine two aspects related to the GTS: (1) its description of the difference between the human and the living more generally and (2) the relationship between self-awareness and sexuality.

a) Human Origin of the Human Dimension

The dialectic of life and living deals with the distinction between life and the consciousness of life. It is an important theme in Hegel. Hyppolite comments: "Awareness of life is something other than life pure and simple, and human existence, like knowledge of life, is a new way of being."[291] In Hegelian thought, the transition from sensory awareness to self-awareness marks the entry into a human existence that makes history possible. Self-awareness, as "independent" consciousness,[292] thus represents an essentially human characteristic. As Hyppolite writes: "It is not man as a biological species that is in question but the emergence at the very heart of life of a being who becomes aware of this life."[293] To become self-conscious, the sensory consciousness of a living creature must pass through another consciousness that is not merely a consciousness of sensation but a consciousness that already recognizes itself as life and that can also recognize sensory consciousness as life. Self-awareness is self-awareness for another self-awareness. This is why the master/slave dialectic involves the

---

291 "Domination/servitude" is the expression adopted by J. Hyppolite in the title of the section presenting this dialectic. (1941/1999), 1:155. In this text, I use the expression *master / slave* which is the form used by Laplanche.

292 G. W. F. Hegel, *Phénoménologie de l'esprit*, vol. 1, trans. Jean Hyppolite (Paris: Aubier, 1999), 155.

293 Hyppolite, Études sur Marx et Hegel, 174.

human dimension of another consciousness as a precondition for its objectification. It therefore has a Copernican dimension: Self-awareness can flow only from another self-awareness. From this point of view, we can draw a parallel between the conditions of objectification of self-consciousness described by Hegel and the process of humanization in the GTS—not in their content, but in their method of thought. Sexualization, as the beginning of the process of humanization, requires the message of another human already humanized, already endowed with an unconscious and carrying sexual fantasies.

This description does not intend to exhaust the different dimensions of the master/slave dialectic. It brings out two elements in the philosophical postulates of the GTS that are related to the rationalist tradition. The first concerns the distinction between the human and the living. The second concerns the rejection of creativism: the assertion that what is sexual comes from the sexual and is not the creation of the subject. One aspect of this rejection is closely associated with the rejection of mysticism. The fantasies that characterizes human sexuality, in the Freudian sense of the sexual, can come only from the fantasy of another. This position is firmly held in Laplanche's theory.

The Human and the Living

We have already seen Laplanche's opposition to the vitalism in which, he says, "the differences between the life of a living being and the 'life' of the spirit all but disappear," as well as his rejection of "vitalist romanticism"[294] and "the obscure presentiment of meaning"[295] in interpretive work. It is a rationalist opposition,

294 Jean Laplanche, "The Wall and the Arcade," in *The Unfinished Copernican Revolution* op. cit. p. 374.

295 Jean Laplanche, "Interpreting (with) Freud," in *The Unfinished Copernican Revolution* op. cit. p. 59.

in the sense of Thomas Mann and Klemperer. This opposition is also reflected in Laplanche's conception of anthropology. He considers the temptation of vitalism as one of the manifestations of Ptolemaic re-centering. Freud translates this vitalism into the idea of the humiliation that the discovery of evolution has inflicted on humans. Laplanche considers placing "evolutionism and a so-called biological humiliation alongside the decenterings introduced by Copernicus and Freud"[296] to be "ambiguous" and "dangerous." "We humans," he writes, "can by no means escape material constraints. On the other hand, the entire history of the species is that of an emancipation from the order of living things. As though fearful of that emancipation, humans are continually situating themselves in a discourse concerning the realm of living things (a 'biology'), and this well before any modern biology. This bio-ideological reference is still far from having said its last word. With regard to every problem confronted by humanity, it is the world of the living, not mankind, that is referred to."[297]

One may wonder if the distinction between the human and the living, echoed in the Hegelian dialectic of self-awareness, also finds an echo in Laplanche's position on Freud's notion of the death drive. He criticizes Freud's "metabiological speculation," opposing it mainly because it entails a mechanism of biological origin and implies a connection—more metaphysical than biological— to "an original naturalness." Freud's death drive is based "on the presupposition that the thesis to prove is the following: The living comes after the nonliving, and as a consequence, the living organism can only tend toward death, since that is what preceded it—a 'living' that arises from and tends to return to what is not

296 Jean Laplanche, "The Unfinished Copernican Revolution," op. cit.
297 Jean Laplanche, "Biologism and Biology," in *Temptation of Biology*, 129.

alive."[298] This rejection is consistent with the delineation of the epistemological field of psychoanalysis as a theory of the soul. For Laplanche, life and death in psychoanalysis are linked to life and death of the soul. Although he uses the expressions "sexual drives of life" and "sexual drives of death," he is careful to recall that "the words life and death do not designate biological death or biological life but their counterparts in the life of the soul and in psychical conflict."[299] The addition of the term "sexual" (e.g., the sexual drives of death) implies that the theory unfolds in the field of the human and not in the more general field of the living.

A similar theme is found in the master/slave dialectic, which, in *The Phenomenology of Mind*, comes after the transition from natural consciousness to self-consciousness, and hence after sensory consciousness—a phenomenon characteristic of living entities— acquires a human form, that of self-consciousness. The struggle to death described in this dialectic does not imply a natural death but rather the preservation of life. In this regard, Hyppolite emphasizes that the movement of recognition that drives the master/slave dialectic implies "the subsistence of nature": Death is not a natural death but, rather, "a disappearing state," which has no "objective side."[300]

What's more, the notion of "subsistence of nature" also highlights the importance that Laplanche gives to the opposition between sexuality and self-preservation and his rejection of any psychoanalytic imperialism. He holds firmly to the notion that psychoanalysis delimits its field of investigation and remains there, while still recognizing both the full legitimacy and complementarity

---

298 Laplanche, "The So-called Death Drive" op. cit. 166

299 Ibid., 170.

300 Hyppolite, Études sur Marx et Hegel, 185, and Hegel, *Phénoménologie de l'esprit*, 155.

of other fields of knowledge.

The Rejection of Creativism

Like self-awareness in the Hegelian dialectic, sexuality as a human characteristic can be formed only from material that is already sexual. This implies the presence of another human who, as a human, is endowed with sexuality. We have, several times, emphasized this point as central to the rationalism of Laplanche's theory. The relationship to Hegelian thinking allows us to reiterate the importance of two aspects that are not always given sufficient attention in commenting on the GTS:

1) The precise nature of the relevant adult/child asymmetry and

2) The need to postulate a time prior to the formation of an unconscious.

The asymmetry described by Laplanche in the fundamental anthropological situation is not based on the child's dependence on the adult but on the absence of a sexual unconsciousness in the child. The dependency of the child is ground on which the sexualized messages are transmitted. In addition, the GTS presupposes that there is a time when the child is within the order of the living, a prepsychoanalytic time, in which the child does not yet have a sexual unconscious. In the same way, Hegel's self-consciousness is not present from the start. There is a time before it comes into existence, the time of sensory consciousness. The requirement for a prepsychoanalytic time and the nature of adult/child asymmetry both fall under the rationalist distinction between fact and law.[301]

---

301 C. Castoriadis, "The Retreat from Autonomy: Post-modernism as Generalized Conformism," *Democracy and Nature* 7, no. 1 (2001).

Here it must be remembered that the GTS does not constitute an empirical model intended to establish a genetic temporality of origin or stages of development.[302] The existence of a prepsychoanalytic time, a time in which the child is a living organism devoid of sexual unconscious, has logical consequences.

Both the source of the sexual unconscious that is already sexual, the human source, and the nonprimal character of the sexual unconscious can be compared to a current in Marxist thought that reaffirms the social character of humans. Although in Marxist theory the natural never disappears completely, its importance within the social fades. In parallel, we could say that in the GTS, naturalness fades away in the face of the sexual. Humanization is the measure of the distance that separates sensory experience from the human experience of the senses. On this subject, Marx writes: "The individual is the social being. His life . . . is an affirmation of social life. . . . The emancipation of all the senses and of all human qualities is an emancipation because these senses and these qualities become human, coming from man and ending in man."[303] This round trip from human to human is reminiscent of the process of sexualization/ reification/disalienation in the GTS. Laplanche develops this line of thinking in *The Temptation of Biology: Freud's Theories of Sexuality*, which meticulously deconstructs and reveals the problems in Freud's characterization of the sexual unconscious as innate and hereditary and does the same for Freud's characterizations of the ego and of narcissism.

Within the GTS, the Copernican requirement accounts for another aspect of the social character of the sexual unconscious and of the ego. This is the issue of the content of thought. We have seen that, in the GTS, the sexual unconscious is primarily a content:

---

302 Laplanche, *Unconscious and the Id.*

303 Marx, *Philosophie,* 151–52.

It is the reified residues of a process of translation, residues that may become linked fantasies. In the same way, the ego consists of translations and forms, which are also more or less linked, of elements that arise from what previously were designified residues. Although the content of the message and the fantasies of the adult that are at its source are metabolized, elaborated, and re-elaborated individually and specifically, they nevertheless come from another human, a social individual whose psychic agencies were formed by the same process. Neither are the contents of psychic agencies created *cum nihilo*, much less ex nihilo, nor do they preexist in a suprahuman world. What's more, they are not already present as such in society or in the socius. They are mediated by another human and metabolized by the subject. This aspect modifies our understanding of social relations and of their mode of reproduction. It is, however, inseparable from the definition of human sexuality as a sexuality whose essence is fantasy.

Sexuality in Psychoanalysis Has a Human Character: Fantasy

In "The So-called Death Drive: A Sexual Drive," Laplanche writes: "I posit the existence of an opposition that is also a superimposition of unbound sexuality (which is erotic) and bound sexuality (which is narcissistic or bound to an object). I should emphasize the following: This opposition is purely human' that is, it is completely informed and oriented by fantasy life. As such, it is the only one with which psychoanalytic practice, which has no other point of impact than fantasy, is concerned."[304] This conclusion follows directly from his definition of the epistemological field of psychoanalysis as a theory of the soul, a definition also within the rationalist tradition. The soul is not a spirit, in the mystical sense, but its contents have the form of a soul. The source of a psychic manifestation can

---

304 Laplanche, "So-called Death Drive," 176.

only be another psychic manifestation; there is no alchemy, no transformation of sensation into ideational content, in the same way that in *The Phenomenology of Mind* there is no automatic passage from consciousness to self-consciousness, experienced as such.

For this reason, Laplanche criticizes the Freudian hypothesis of coexcitation, a hypothesis that attributes the genesis of the sexual drive to an excitation provoked by nonsexual sources. He asks: If, as in the hypothesis of coexcitation, one starts "from a sort of vital, objective sadomasochism, which is never anything but the struggle of two great biological forces, how can one trace the origins of the masochistic *fantasy*? Could biological drives put on borrowed psychical clothes, rather as in Susan Isaacs's conception of the nature of fantasy?"[305] How could a bodily disturbance or a purely sensory phenomenon give rise to a mental phenomenon including the affect felt as an affect? This criticism is connected to a fundamental problem of rationalism to which we have returned several times: the need to account for the origin of the contents of a given. The direct transformation of a sensory phenomenon into a thought—into the content of a thought—implies transcendence of the sensory, which would then mean that sensory phenomena have a meaning prior to the sensation itself. Such a position is mystical. Laplanche points this out:

> Here, on the question of fantasy, we should mark
> the point where things come to a halt. Fantasy is
> brought in only in a secondary way, as a sort of epi-
> phenomenon, the psychical adornment of a purely
> biological process. To put fantasy back at the origin
> is to put the whole process and its derivation back
> on its feet. It is impossible to start from a pure ero-
> togenic masochism if one is to understand anything

---

305 Laplanche, "Masochism and the General Theory of Seduction," op. cit.

at all about masochism. Its true derivation can start
only from the genuinely nonspeculative domain of
psychoanalysis: that of fantasy, in its originary link
to excitation and orgasm.[306]

By using the expression "to put the whole process and its
derivation back on its feet," Laplanche alludes to a formulation of
Marx on the dialectic, which calls for removing the mysticism that
Hegel introduced.[307]

b) Sexuality and Self-Awareness

By placing fantasy at the origin of the process of sexualization,
the GTS places psychoanalysis in a relay. It is not a substitute for
other sciences that study the organic, psychological, and perceptual
aspects of development or that study the processes of maturation
and other aspects of thought and action, no more than is sociology,
philosophy, or ethics. It accounts for the formation of a specifically
human reality, psychic reality, an "invasive" reality that must be
considered an essential dimension of behavior and the human
condition. The GTS implies that "the sexual apparatus of the soul
tends to take as its own, to invade, and to appropriate the domain
of psychological reality, which in principle is independent, but in
the human being, it is independent only in an abstract way."[308]

This has implications for the conception of subjectivity. The
concept of subjectivity has taken on considerable importance in

---

306 Ibid. [Translation modified.]

307 Here is the quote from Marx: "The mystifying side of Hegelian dialectic I
criticized nearly thirty years ago, at a time when it was still the fashion. [...] The
mystification which dialectic suffers in Hegel's hands, by no means prevents him
from being the first to present its general form of working in a comprehensive and
conscious manner. With him it is standing on its head. It must be turned right side
up again, if you would discover the rational kernel within the mystical shell. " Karl
Marx, afterword of the German edition of *Capital*.

308 Laplanche, "Forces at Play in Psychical Conflict," 114. [Translation modified.]

contemporary psychoanalysis, but this has not much deepened the theorization of subjectivity's links with the agencies of metapsychology.[309]

Subjectivity is not a psychoanalytic concept. Laplanche systematically avoids referring to it. Nor does he refer to the notion of the subject. He repeatedly insists that psychoanalysis is not a philosophy of the subject. Indeed, from a rationalist perspective, psychoanalysis, which is born by exploding the idea of subject, puts the philosophical use of this concept into question in order to include the conflictual dimension introduced by psychic reality and the sexual unconscious.

However, as Laplanche writes, one cannot deny that there are connections between the psychic agencies of psychoanalysis and subjectivity to the extent that these agencies—id, ego, ideal agencies, and superego—"take over" the activities of the soul. Moreover, even if it is true that one could not understand subjectivity without taking into consideration "the sexual apparatus of the soul," it is equally true that the apparatus of the soul cannot completely define subjectivity. Subjectivity involves other dimensions, particularly sociological and moral ones. But these too cannot be understood independently of psychical reality that, in a large part, constitutes their material cause. The agencies of the apparatus of the soul have content. They "can be conceived only in terms of their origin: the impact on a developing biological organism of enigmatic messages emanating from the other."[310] The contents of the ego and of the sexual unconscious are thus directly related to subjectivity in the philosophical sense of the term, including in the sphere of decision and action.

---

309 This statement must be nuanced with regard to the Lacanian orientation, in particular Lacan himself, who has dealt a lot with the question of the subject, from a perspective linked to castration and the phylogenetic lineage.

310 Laplanche, "Forces at Play in Psychical Content," 115

Hegel's account of the passage from consciousness to self-consciousness bears resemblance to the passage, in Laplanche's theory, of the nonthetic consciousness of the prepsychoanalytic child, to the humanized consciousness that, because of primal repression, includes a sexual apparatus of the soul. Without making a term-by-term equation—after all, the two theories move on different epistemological levels—one can use the parallel with the dialectic of self-awareness to highlight some contributions of the GTS to the understanding of subjectivity, a notion that is, moreover, essential for building bridges between psychoanalysis and the human sciences.

For Hegel, self-awareness is what makes history possible. To look for the conditions of self-awareness is thus to seek "the conditions for the very existence of man."[311] From this point of view, self-awareness is a possibility of subjectivity.[312] Could we, on this basis, see a meeting point between the ego of the GTS and self-awareness? Although the two belong to distinct registers, they partially restore overlapping realities. "A consciousness . . . essentially consists in a coherent ego that temporalizes itself," Laplanche writes.[313] The formation of the ego would thus be a precondition for self-consciousness. Yet, as we have seen, the formation of the ego is dependent on the primal repression. As a result, sexualization is also a necessary condition for self-awareness, and therefore, it constitutes a condition of possibility for subjectivity, at least insofar as one accepts the links between subjectivity and self-awareness.

---

311 Hyppolite, *Études sur Marx et Hegel*, 175.

312 In this chapter, the question of subjectivity is taken up in the philosophical sense—that is, in a sense that includes several meanings. A. De Libera, *Archéologie du sujet*, 2 vols. (Paris: Vrin, 2007–08). In principle, psychological subjectivity can exist independently of repression. But in the human, it cannot be conceived of as independent of psychic reality that itself is constituted by repression.

313 Laplanche, "So-called Death Drive," 174.

The issue of subjectivity arises in connection with transformation. The relation that the GTS establishes between sexualization and subjectivity, as well as the parallel that can be observed between this theory and the dialectic of self-consciousness, provokes reflections on the role of masochism in subjectivity, and on the other hand, it calls into question the traditional understanding of the relationship between subjectivity and objectivity.

Masochism and Subjectivity

Laplanche points out that "the so-called death drive is effectively a 'pure culture' of alterity that we find in the deepest layers of the unconscious. Doubtless these deepest residues are intimately related to sadomasochism,"[314] a kinship accentuated by their exclusion from the category of communication. "A man with whom we cannot communicate creates fear," wrote Albert Camus. Without falling into anthropomorphism, one can say that the fact that the unbound contents of the unconscious escape the sphere of communication defines their mode of action: that of attack. What's more, we also know that some of the content of the ego is also related to masochism.[315] The attraction that masochism exercises may itself be indebted to unconscious fantasy. To situate masochistic fantasy in the very heart not only of subjectivity but also of a possible movement of subjectivation constitutes a significant contribution of the GTS to thought in the social domain.

The place masochism occupies in the formation of subjectivity is prefigured in the master/slave dialectic and its location in Hegel's *The Phenomenology of Mind*. This dialectic constitutes a metaphor for consciousness's relationships of dependence and independence, for its capacity to objectify itself not only in relation to itself but

---

314 Ibid., 174.

315 Hélène Tessier, in Marzano, *Dictionnaire de la violence*.

also in relation to others.[316]

The introduction of the master/slave dialectic at this precise moment of the theorization of self-consciousness has an enigmatic dimension. Without extrapolating from the thought of Hegel, examining this dialectic in the light of the GTS can make it appear as an intuitive expression of the centrality of masochism in becoming human—not only in the process of subjectivation, but also in the process of objectification. This centrality then raises the question of the attraction of domination, which would appear transversely in all spheres of life. In a commentary on *The Phenomenology of Mind* of Hegel, we find a rather astonishing reflection on this subject: "In

his theoretical life as well as in his practical life, would man be condemned to sadomasochism?"

Dialectic, Negation, and Subjectivation

By asserting that the enigmatic message, carrying the adult's unconscious sexual fantasy, is the triggering element of the drive to translate in the child, the GTS places the imbalance introduced by nonsense at the origin of the movement of making sense. Thus, the designified, which resists symbolization, becomes the engine pushing for translation and signifying connection.

This position is close to the idea of contradiction as the engine of history. There are two reasons that it is a dialectical position. On the one hand, it supposes a passage from the subject to the object and from the object to the subject, which, as Merleau-Ponty pointed out, constitutes the foundation of dialectics.[317] This passage is made thanks to the fundamental anthropological situation, in particular thanks to the message.[318] On the other hand, the action of negation

---

316 Hegel, *Phénoménologie de l'esprit*, 155.

317 M. Merleau-Ponty, *Les aventures de la dialectique* (Paris: Gallimard, 1955), 48n1.

318 Even if the notions of subject and object are not psychoanalytic notions, we

is added to it. As a result, this position is related to the rationalist tradition of dialectics and its goal of transformation as described by Marx: "In its mystified form, dialectic became the fashion in Germany, because it seemed to transfigure and to glorify the existing state of things. In its rational form it is a scandal and abomination to bourgeoisdom and its doctrinaire professors, because it includes in its comprehension and affirmative recognition of the existing state of things, at the same time also, the recognition of the negation of that state, of its inevitable breaking up; because it regards every historically developed social form as in fluid movement, and therefore takes into account its transient nature not less than its momentary existence; because it lets nothing impose upon it, and is in its essence critical and revolutionary."[319]

The transformation of reality is the central problem of dialectical thought.[320] The GTS is no exception. Thus, in his description of the ego, Laplanche emphasizes the importance of "the identificatory contributions and successive rearrangements that come to enrich and dialecticize that agency."[321] In the same way, his conception of the transformative action and of analytic treatment implies a movement of translation/detranslation, which testifies to the "transitory configuration" of the ego and, to a certain extent, the related contents found in the unconscious. The movement of translation constitutes a work of subjectivation that is carried out according to a dialectical temporality, the temporality of après-

---

can refer to them here since we are talking about the description of dialectics in the philosophical sense. On the other hand, the movement of the object in the subject in the fundamental anthropological situation is not limited to the simultaneous presence of the adult and the child but resides, above all, in the message. We will come back to this in the next section.

319 Marx, afterword to the German edition of Capital, 511 **check standard english translation**

320 Lukács, *Histoire et conscience de classe.*

321 Laplanche, "Forces at Play in Psychical Conflict," 118.

coup.[322] Laplanche writes: "[T]o subjectivize in analysis—we know that this process is inseparable from a certain dialectical conception of temporality that, with Freud, we call 'après-coup' and that designates a particular modality of human symbolization."[323]

Endogenous/Exogenous and Subjective/Objective Relations

Laplanche does not refer to the notion of subjectivity to describe transformation. He uses the verb "to subjectivize" to refer to an action of the soul that goes beyond the subject/object dichotomy, the dichotomy around which debates over the truth have often crystallized. Without dwelling on it, let's recall that in particular, but not exclusively, in Anglo-Saxon psychoanalysis there is still a significant debate about whether subjective experience is true in itself or whether its truth must be confirmed by external reality. Posing the question that way amounts to assimilating psychoanalysis to a theory of knowledge.

The question of truth does not boil down to the "*adequatio rei et intellectus*"[324]—in other words, to the truth of knowledge. In the Hegelian dialectic, truth results from an identity between subject and object. "With self-consciousness, we have entered the homeland of truth," wrote Hegel.[325] This is where the struggle for recognition comes in: "Self-awareness is in itself and for itself when and because of self-awareness for self-awareness."[326] Existential philosophy has fought this position. On this subject Kierkegaard wrote: "The idea proper to the System is that of the subject-object, of the unity of thought and of being. Existence, on the other hand,

322 Laplanche, "Temporality and Translation," 220.

323 Jean Laplanche, *"The Psychoanalytic Treatment of Psychotic Conditions,"* in *The Unfinished Copernican Revolution.*

324 Schüssler, *La question de la verité.*

325 Hegel, *Phénoménologie de l'esprit*, 146.

326 Ibid., 155.

is precisely what separates them."[327] For Søren Kierkegaard, "subjectivity, interiority, is truth."[328]

Because of its relation to rationalism, the GTS does not fall on the side of existential philosophy or on the side of Hegelian dialectics. It is close to Marxist thought, for which, as we have already seen, "the unity of subject and object" is, above all, activity.[329] In Laplanche's theory of seduction, the activities in question take the form of message and translation.

These two activities modify the traditional understanding of the relation between inner and outer and between subjective and objective. The subject and the object meet in these activities. The message conveys a double alterity, a double dialectical movement of the subject in the object. It has an external otherness, since, from the point of view of the receiver, the message comes from the other; and yet it also has an internal otherness: The message is not confused with the one who emits it. It is objectified in relation to the sender.

Moreover, translation is also a process that does not recognize a tight seal between what is objective and what is subjective. For the author of the original text, the text is objectified. For the translator, the text has an external otherness. But in the translation activity, "the translator does not appear as the mere servant of objective content." He also expresses himself.[330]

The theory of translation is an essential source for Laplanche's anthropology. Through "the movement of potentiation" that it entails, translation is at once an interpretation and a transformation.[331]

327 Søren Kierkegaard, 1846, in *L'existence*, ed. J. Brun, trans. H. Tisseau (Paris: PUF, 1972), 49.

328 Ibid., 63.

329 Lukács, *History and Class Consciousness*, 185.

330 Berman, *L'épreuve de l'étranger*, 233.

331 Ibid., 175.

Conclusion Anthropology
and Translation

Translation and the category of the message are tightly linked to the rationalism of Laplanche's theorizing. They are also integral parts of his conception of sexuality and seduction but are often wrongly treated as epiphenomena. Although Laplanche did not directly refer to it, it must be emphasized that the general theory of seduction bears a similar name to a philosophical theory of translation, the "general theory of translation" (a phrase used by Berman to characterize the theory of translation of the German romantics),[332] which occupied a central place in romantic thought. However, the GTS does not fit into or overlap with all aspects of the general theory of translation. For example, it does not incorporate the romantic theme according to which everything is translatable and can be translated into any other language. Indeed, the untranslatable and the untranslated play a major role in Laplanche's theory. On the other hand, as far as its aim is concerned, it is close to the rationalist side of the general theory of translation. This consists of the attempt to give a speculative foundation to transformation, to the capacity of the contents and forms of thought to transform themselves. Laplanche's theory attempts to describe "the ontological area of the transformable, the convertible."[333] It is difficult to discuss the connection of Laplanche's theory to rationalism without addressing the status of the drive to translate.[334] The drive to translate could, wrongly, be seen as an irrationalist concept. What is this drive—a Freudian term, at least in the context

---

332 Antoine Berman, *L'épreuve de l'étranger* (Paris: Gallimard, 1984), 110.

333 Ibid., 137.

334 Jean Laplanche, *The Unfinished Copernican Revolution* op. cit. and Jean Laplanche, *Between Seduction and Inspiration : Man* op. cit.

of psychoanalysis—an additional drive that would be added to the other drives of psychoanalytic theory and thus claim to preexist the sexual drive? That is not the case. In Laplanche's theory, the drive to translate refers to the ethical basis of his conception of psychoanalysis. It is at the source of his anthropology. It does not distance his theory from the rationalist tradition, but, indeed, it constitutes an essential link in the relationship between rationalism and the GTS.

Inspired by Novalis, the phrase "drive to translate" is used by Walter Benjamin.[335] It defines the metaphysical aim of translation. Antoine Berman also takes the phrase "drive to translate"[336] or, sometimes, "drive of translating"[337] to designate this aim: what pushes the translator to seek "a 'truth' lying beyond natural languages."[338] In the GTS, the notion of the drive to translate covers three realities: the compulsion to translate, the drive's relationship with the sexual unconscious, and translation itself. The three are closely related. As we have seen, the compulsion to translate has its source in the enigmatic aspect of message the adult sends to the child or, in other words and more precisely, in the internal imbalance that characterizes these messages. This compulsion therefore has a drive aspect, since the imbalance is the result of the sexual aspect of the adult's message and consequently of the excitement associated with the unconscious fantasy that infiltrates the message. The origin of the sexual side of the drive to translate is neither mythical

---

335 In 1923, in the preface to his translation of Charles Baudelaire's *Tableaux parisiens*, "The Task of the Translator," Benjamin speaks of the "pure drive to translate" and the "pure aim of translation." L. Curreri, "Commentaires polémiques sur la théorie de la traduction," *Le journal de Babel* 22 (November 2006), www.babel.ulg. ac/ bulletin/n22/cp.pdf.

336 Berman, *L'épreuve de l'étranger*, 283.

337 Ibid., 21.

338 Ibid.

nor biological: That adults have a sexual unconscious that resists everyday meaning is the heart of the discovery of psychoanalysis. As Laplanche writes, "[P]sychoanalysis has taught us that the adult is inhabited by an unconscious, that is sexual . . . and is constituted by representations and fantasies that infiltrate behaviors."[339] Thus, the compulsion, or drive, to translate "derives its power not from the translator but from the thing left untranslated or inadequately translated, that thing always demanding a better translation."[340]

Translation, the third reality covered by the expression "the drive to translate," must also be the subject of our reflection concerning the expression's connection to rationalist thought. Why translation? In addition to situating the origin of the unconscious in the frame of interhuman communication, as used by Laplanche, what does the theory of translation contribute to the GTS? Why would the human being be a translator? In the GTS, the drive to translate and the reference to translation contained in that concept remain faithful to the delimitation of the epistemological field of psychoanalysis. The drive to translate, as well as the possibility of translating and the ability to translate, does not belong to developmental psychology or to cognitive science. Laplanche argues that psychoanalysis intervenes as a discipline while the living organism that is the infant is already endowed with the biological, physiological, and psychological properties necessary for its maturation. The conception of what constitutes a human in the process of becoming is not limited to the organic and psychological components. It also includes philosophical presuppositions. The reference to translation that underlies the notion of a drive to translate reflects an ontological position.

---

339 Jean Laplanche, "Goals of the Psychoanalytic Process," in *Between Seduction and Inspiration: Man*, 191–92.

340 Jean Laplanche, "Temporality and Translation," op. cit. 418

Although this example may seem far removed from psychoanalytic theory—in fact, it is – one can draw a parallel between the nature of the drive to translate in the GTS and the notion of equality in the doctrine of human rights. The purpose of this comparison is not to show that the GTS speaks of human rights but to highlight the role of the drive to translate as a conception of man. "Mortals are equal," Voltaire wrote, "it is not birth, it is virtue alone that makes the difference." In fact, however, nothing is less true physically, psychologically, intellectually, and socially. To assert the equality of all in law, and especially in dignity, constitutes a philosophical position, or a political one, which has no empirical basis. The drive to translate is part of the same cultural wealth. It places the search for meaning at the heart of the definition of the human. Laplanche notably refers to this when he asserts that instinctual renunciation is not an imperative of the superego. This renunciation, he writes, "far from being a dictate of the superego, is the cultural destiny of every human being—namely, to translate and put into narrative form for himself the messages of the other, including their most enigmatic sexual aspects."[341] The reference to translation confers a moral framework on the GTS. The ethics of translation unfolds beyond empirical languages. It implies the idea of a language, or a formulation, toward which one can tend and that could always be improved, always be more true.[342] Like this theory of translation, the GTS assumes a moral postulate: that of the possibility of "a better [...] more equitable life according to the spirit" (Thomas Mann, already quoted).

This aspect is related to the rationalist tradition that links reason and emancipation. Emancipation involves a transcendent

---

341 Jean Laplanche, "Incest and Infantile Sexuality," in *Freud and the Sexual*, 302. [Translation modified.]

342 Berman, *L'épreuve de l'étranger*.

dimension: It presumes that one recognizes, in law, the possible existence of more emancipated forms of life. The GTS is based on this postulate. Just like the drive to translate, it does not come from empirical considerations. It constitutes an axiological position. It is close to the Aristotelian conception of virtue: The category of good relates to seeing the possibility of an emancipatory transformation in each individual existence as well as in social relations. Such a position also echoes the thought of Klemperer, who, in the face of the terror that things could never improve, wrote: "[B]ut reason always commands one to say to oneself: but perhaps if—and to act in consequence of that 'if.' When we have no choice, we do what reason commands."[343]

In this context, reason becomes a principle of resistance. This principle is at work in Laplanche's thought, a thought that concedes nothing to arguments from authority.

It is here that the question of the choice of a metapsychological theory comes into play. It is not a given that every psychoanalytic theory is compatible with the belief that psychoanalysis has, in its essence, a goal of emancipation. The aim of emancipation is not limited to treatment. To be compatible with the hypothesis of a transformative aim, a metapsychological theory must describe a soul capable of transformation. In addition, to meet the conditions of possibility of emancipation, it must be based on principles that safeguard autonomy. Thus, it must meet two seemingly contradictory criteria: the conditions for safeguarding a specific autonomy, respectful of each person's individual history, and, at the same time, the ability to postulate a freer form of the life of the soul, a freedom to which everyone is entitled to aspire.

In the form of drive renunciation, the GTS presupposes a duty to free oneself from "the constraint of fantasy" and, more

---

343 Victor Klemperer, vol. 1 (2000), 391.

concretely, from the masochistic fantasy. The GTS is a response to a demand for truth Marx evoked when he wrote: "To call on [people] to give up their illusions about their condition is to call on them to give up a condition that requires illusions."[344] It formulates this requirement not as an injunction—such an injunction would be illusory—but as a search for the conditions of possibility of the resumption of a movement of translation favoring less alienated, more encompassing translations. The GTS's opposition to the irrationalist tendencies of Freudian and post-Freudian theories constitutes a true confidence in psychoanalysis, confidence that psychoanalysis can bring understanding to human behaviors and transformation in the direction of a freer life. Therefore, its rationalism is a humanism, "a political stance, an attitude of revolt against all that . . . denatures (*entwürdige*) the idea of man."[345]

---

344 Karl Marx, "A Contribution to the Critique of Hegel's Philosophy of Right," in *Philosophie*, 91.

345 The Magic Mountain. Here is the original text: "*damit sei er auch Politik, sei er auch Rebellion gegen alles, was Die Idee Menschens . . . entwürdige.*"

BIBLIOGRAPHY OF WORKS BY JEAN LAPLANCHE

The following is incomplete is several respects. A complete list of Laplanche's writings, collected and uncollected, of all translations of his work and of all video and audio recordings is being prepared and will be available on the web site of the Fondation Laplanche.

1960 *L'Inconscient : une étude psychanalytique* in collaboration with Serge Leclaire. Presented at the VI Colloque de Bonneval. Proceedings of the Colloque *L'Inconscient* were published by Desclée de Brouwer, Paris, 1966 in a volume containing other interventions by Laplanche.

>   Republished in *Problématiques IV. L'inconscient et le ça.* Paris: P.U.F., 1981.

>   E: *The Unconscious: A Psychoanalytic Study* Trans. Patrick Coleman. Yale French Studies, no. 48, 1972.

1961 *Hölderlin et la question du père. Paris: P.U.F., 1961.*

>   E: *Hölderlin and the Question of the Father . Ed. and trans. Luke Carson. Introduction by Rainer Nägele. Victoria, BC: ELS Editions, 2007.*

1964 *Fantasme originaire, fantasmes des origines, origines du fantasme* in collaboration with J.-B. Pontalis. Les Temps Modernes, #215, Volume 19, April 1964.

>   1985 Republished in the series *Textes du XXe siècle* with a new introduction by the authors. Paris: Hachette, 1985.

E: ***Primal Fantasy, Fantasies of Origins, Origins of Fantasy***, trans. Jonathan. *Laplanche*, Dominique Scarfone, New York: The Unconscious in Translation, 2015.

Fantasy and the Origins of Sexuality; International Journal of Psychoanalysis, vol. 49, 1968. [Reprinted in *Formations of Fantasy*, ed. Victor Burgin et al, Methuen, 1986; also reprinted in *Unconscious Phantasy*, ed. Ricardo Steiner, London: Karnac Books, 2003].

1967   *Vocabulaire de la psychanalyse* in collaboration with J.-B. Pontalis. Paris: P.U.F.

E: ***The Language of Psycho-Analysis***. Trans. D. Nicholson-Smith. New York: Norton, 1973.

1970   *Vie et mort en psychanalyse*. Paris: Flammarion, 1970.

2nd edition 1971, includes *Dérivation des entités psychanalytiques*

E: ***Life and Death in Psychoanalysis***. Trans. J. Mehlman. Baltimore: Johns Hopkins University Press, 1976. Includes *Derivation of Psychoanalytic Entities*

1970-73   Lectures given at the *Sorbonne-Université de Paris VII,* for his course within the UER des Sciences Humaines, published in the journal *Psychanalyse à l'université;* and then in ***Problématiques I. L'angoisse***. Paris: P.U.F., 1980.

1970-1971 : L' « Angst » dans la névrose
1971-1972 : L'angoisse dans la topique

1972-1973 : L'angoisse morale

1973-75 Lectures given at the *Sorbonne-Université de Paris VII*, for his course within the UER des Sciences Humaines, published in the journal *Psychanalyse à l'université*; ***and then in Problématiques II. Castration. Symbolisations.*** Paris: P.U.F., 1980.

> 1973-1974 : La castration, ses précurseurs et son destin
> 1974-1975 : Symbolisations

> E: *Extract:* **Lecture 20 May, 1975.** Trans. Arthur Goldhammer. *Literary Debate : Texts and Contexts*, Ed. Dennis Hollier and Jeffrey Mehlman. New York: The New Press, 1999.

1975-77 Lectures given at the *Sorbonne-Université de Paris VII*, for his course within the UER des Sciences Humaines, published in the journal *Psychanalyse à l'université*; and then in ***Problématiques III. La sublimation.*** Paris: P.U.F., 1980.

> 1975-1976 : Pour situer la sublimation
> 1976-1977 : Faire dériver la sublimation

> E: Extract: **To Situate Sublimation.** Trans. Richard Miller. *October*, No. 28, Spring, 1984.

1977-79 Lectures given at the *Sorbonne-Université de Paris VII*, for his course within the UER des Sciences Humaines, published in the journal *Psychanalyse à l'université*; and then in ***Problématiques IV. L'Inconsient et le Ça.*** Paris: P.U.F., 1981.

1977-1978 : La référence à l'inconscient

1978-1979 : Problématique du ça

E: ***The Unconscious and the Id*** , Trans. Luke Thurston with Lindsay Watson, London: Rebus Press, 1999.

1979-84   Lectures given at the *Sorbonne-Université de Paris VII*, for his course within the UER des Sciences Humaines, published in the journal *Psychanalyse à l'université*; and then in ***Problématiques V. Le baquet – Transcendance du transfert.*** Paris: P.U.F., 1987.

1979-1980 : Le psychanalyste et son baquet

1980-1981 : Le descriptif et le prescriptif

1983-1984 : La transcendance du transfer

1987   ***Nouveaux fondements pour 1a psychanalyse.*** Paris: P.U.F., 1987.

E: ***New Foundations for Psychoanalysis,*** trans. David Macey, Oxford: Basil Blackwell, 1989.

New Foundations for Psychoanalysis , trans. Jonathan House and Robert Stein, New York: The Unconscious in Translation, 2016.

1989   ***Traduire Freud.*** In collaboration with A. Bourguignon, P. Cotet, F. Roberts. Paris: P.U.F., 1989.

E: Extract: **Translating Freud,** trans. Maev de la Guardia and Bertrand Vichyn, in *Translating Freud,* ed. Darius Gray Ornston, New Haven: Yale University Press, 1992.

1989-90   Lectures given at the *Sorbonne-Université de Paris VII*, for his course within the UER des Sciences Humaines, published in the journal *Psychanalyse à l'université*; and then in ***Problématiques VI. L'après-coup.*** Paris: P.U.F., 2006.

1989-1990 : La « Nachträglichkeit » dans l'après-coup

1991-92 Lectures given at the *Sorbonne-Université de Paris VII,* for his course within the UER des Sciences Humaines, published in the journal *Psychanalyse à l'université;* and then in ***Problématiques VII : Le fourvoiement biologisant de la sexualité chez Freud suivi de Biologisme et biologie.*** Paris: P.U.F., initially published in 1993 by Synthélabo .

E: The Temptation of Biology: Freud's Theories of Sexuality. Trans. Donald Nicholson-Smith. New York: The Unconscious in Translation, 2015.

E: Extract: **Exigency and Going-Astray.** Trans. Vincent Ladmiral and Nicholas Ray. *Psychoanalysis, Culture and Society*, 11, 2006, pp. 164189.

1992 *La révolution copernicienne inachevée (Travaux 1967-1992).* Paris: Aubier, 1992.

E. The Unfinished Copernican Revolution. Trans. Luke Thurstson, New York: The Unconscious in Translation, 2020.

English translations of works contained in this volume

1968 **Interpreting [with] Freud** (*Interpréter [avec] Freud).* Trans. Vincent Ladmiral and Nicholas Ray, *Psychoanalysis, Culture* *and Society*. vol. 11, 2006.

1979 **A Metapsychology put to the Test of Anxiety** *(Une métapsychologie à lépreuve de l'angoisse)*. *International Journal of Psychoanalysis*, vol. 62, 1981.

1984 **The Drive and its Object-source: its fate in the transference** *(La pulsion et son objet-source. Son destin dans le transfer)*.

T rans. Martin Stanton *Jean Laplanche: Seduction, Trans lation and the Drives*, ed. John Fletcher and Martin Stanton, London: Institute of Contemporary Arts, 1992.

T rans. Leslie Hill. *Essays on Otherness*, ed. John Fletcher, London: Routledge, 1999.

1987 **Specificity of Terminological Problems in the Translation of Freud** *(Spécificité des problèmes terminologiques dans la traduc tion de Freud)*. *International Review of Psychoanalysis*, vol. 18, 1991.

1988 **The Wall and the Arcade** *(Le mur et l'arcade)*. Trans. Martin Stanton. Op. cit.

1989 **Psycholanalysis, Time and Translation** *(Temporalité et trad uction. Pour une remise au travail de la philosophie du temps)*. Trans. Martin Stanton. Op. cit. New translation, Luke Thurston, in *Aprèscoup* ed. Jonathan House, New York, The Unconscious in Translation, 2017.

1990 **Implantation, Intromission** *(Implation, intromission)*. Trans Luke Thurston, *Essays on Otherness*, ed. John Fletcher, London: Routledge, 1999.

1990   **Time and the Other** *(Le temps et l'autre)*. Trans. Luke
        Thurston. *Essays on Otherness*, ed. John Fletcher, London:
        Routledge, 1999. Revised translation by Luke Thurston
        in Aprèscoup ed. Jonathan House, New York, The
        Unconscious in Translation, 2017.

        Interpretation Between Determinism and Hermeneutics:
        A Restatement of the Problem *(L'interprétation entre*
        déterminisme et herméneutique: une nouvelle position de la
        question) Trans. Philip Slotkin. Essays on Otherness, ed.
        John Fletcher, London: Routledge, 1999.

        Masochism and the General Theory of Seduction
        (Masochisme et théorie de la séduction généralisée). Trans. Luke
        Thurston. *Essays on Otherness*, ed. John Fletcher, London:
        Routledge, 1999.

1992   **Transference: its Provocation by the Analyst** *(Du transfert*
        : sa provocation par l'analyste). Trans. Luke Thurston. *Essays*
        on Otherness, ed. John Fletcher, London: Routledge, 1999.

1992   **The Unfinished Copernican Revolution** *(La révolution*
        copernicienne inachevée). Trans. Luke Thurston *Essays on*
        Otherness, ed. John Fletcher, London: Routledge, 1999.

1997   *"The Theory of Seduction and the Problem of the Other."* Trans.
        Luke Thurston. *International Journal of Psychoanalysis*, vol.
        78, no. 4, 1997.

1998   *"From the Restricted to the Generalized Theory of Seduction."*
        In *Seduction, Suggestion, Psychoanalysis*. Ed. Jose Corveleyn
        and Philippe Van Haute. Leuven University Press and
        Duquesne University Press, 1998.

1999 *Entre séduction et inspiration : L'Homme.* Paris: P.U.F., 1999.

E: *Between Seduction and Inspiration.* Trans. Jeffrey Mehlman, New York: The Unconscious in Translation, 2015

E: Other English translations of works contained in this volume

1992 *Notes on Afterwardsness.* Trans. Martin Stanton *Jean Laplanche: Seduction, Translation and the Drives*, ed. John Fletcher and Martin Stanton, London: Institute of Contemporary Arts, 1992. Taken from a recorded conversation with Martin Stanton. Later augmented by Laplanche and published with the same title in *Essays on Otherness*, ed. John Fletcher, London: Routledge, 1999. Also, in a French version in *Entre séduction et inspiration : l'homme.* Paris, PUF 1999

1992 **The Unfinished Copernican Revolution** *(La révolution copernicienne inachevée)*. Trans. Luke Thurston *Essays on Otherness*, ed. John Fletcher, London: Routledge, 1999.

1992 **Seduction, Persecution, Revelation** *(Séduction, persécution, révélation)*. Trans. Philip Slotkin. *The International Journal of Psychoanalysis*, vol. 76, no. 4, 1996

1994 **Psychoanalysis as Anti-hermeneutics** *(La psychanalyse comme anti-herméneutique)*. Trans. Luke Thurston. *Radical Philosophy*, no. 79, Sept./Oct., 1996.

1995 **The So-Called 'Death-Drive': a Sexual Drive** *(La soi-disant pulsion de mort : une pulsion sexuelle)*. Trans. Luke

Thurston. *The Death-Drive*. Ed. Rob Weatherill, London: Rebus Press, 1999. Reprinted in *The British Journal of Psychotherapy*, vol. 20, no. 4, 2004.

1996   **Aims of the Psychoanalytic Process** *(Buts du processus psychanalytique)*. *Journal of European Psychoanalysis*, no. 5, Spring/ Fall, 1997.

1996   **Psychoanalysis: Myths and Theories** (La psychanalyse: mythes et théorie.) Trans. *Psychoanalytic Quarterly*, vol. 77, no. 3, 2003.

1998   **Narrativity and Hermeneutics: some propositions** *(Narrativité et herméneutique: quelque propositions.)* Trans. John Fletcher. *New Formations*, no. 48, Winter, 2002/3

1999   **Sublimation   and/or Inspiration** (Sublimation et/ou inspiration.) Trans. John Fletcher. *New Formations*, no. 48, Winter, 2002-3

2006   *Problématiques VI: L'après-coup*

   E: Après-coup, trans. Jonathan House, New York: The Unconscious in Translation, 2017.

Sexual : La sexualité élargie au sens freudien 2000-2006. Paris: P.U.F.

   E: *Freud and the Sexual: Essays 2000-2006*, ed. John Fletcher; trans. John Fletcher, Jonathan House, Nicholas Ray. New York: The Unconscious in Translation, (IPB) 2011

   E: Other English translations of works contained in this volume

2000   **Sexuality and Attachment in Metapsychology** *(Sexualité et* *l'attachement dans la metapsychologie.)* Trans. Susan Fairfield. *Infantile Sexuality and Attachment.* Ed. Daniel Widlöcher. New York: Other Press, 2002.

2000   **Closing and Opening of the Dream: Must Chapter VII be Rewritten?** *(Rêve et communication : faut-il réécrire me chapitre VII?)* Trans. Mira Reinberg and Thomas Pepper. *Dreams of Interpretation: A Century down the Royal Road.* Ed. Catherin Liu et al. Minneapolis: University of Minnesota Press, 2007.

2003   **Gender, Sex, and the Sexual** *(Le genre, le sexe, le sexual.)"* Trans.Susan Fairfield. *Gender and Sexuality*, vol. 8, no. 2, 2007.

www.ingramcontent.com/pod-product-compliance
Lightning Source LLC
Chambersburg PA
CBHW060228030426
42335CB00014B/1372